Verbal Workout for the SAT

Verbal Workout for the SAT

Second Edition

By Geoff Martz

Random House, Inc.
New York

www.PrincetonReview.com

The Independent Education Consultants Association recognizes The Princeton Review as a valuable resource for high school and college students applying to college and graduate school.

Princeton Review Publishing, L.L.C.
2315 Broadway
New York, NY 10024
E-mail: booksupport@review.com

ISBN: 0-375-76176-4

Editor: Russell Kahn
Production Editor: Maria Dente
Production Coordinator: Robert McCormack

Manufactured in the United States of America.

9 8 7 6 5 4

Second Edition

ACKNOWLEDGMENTS

Thanks to Lee Elliott, Kristin Fayne-Mulroy, Chris Kensler, Marcia Lerner, Meher Khambata, Mia Barron, Jeannie Yoon, Jane Lacher, and all the Princeton Review teachers whose ingenuity and hard work made this book possible. For additional production and editing help, thanks to Jeff Rubenstein, Andrea Paykin, Mike Freedman, Andy Lutz, Cynthia Brantley, Julian Ham, Andrew Dunn, Debbie Guest, Clayton Harding, Kathleen Standard, Christopher D. Scott, Christopher J. Thomas, John Bergdahl, Jefferson Nichols, Joe Cavallaro, Sara Kane, Ramsey Silberberg, Matthew Clark, Illeny Maaza, Maria Dente, and Carol Slominski. And special thanks to Dinica Quesada for designing the flash cards.

Special thanks to Adam Robinson, who conceived of and perfected the Joe Bloggs approach to standardized tests, and many of the other successful techniques used by The Princeton Review.

CONTENTS

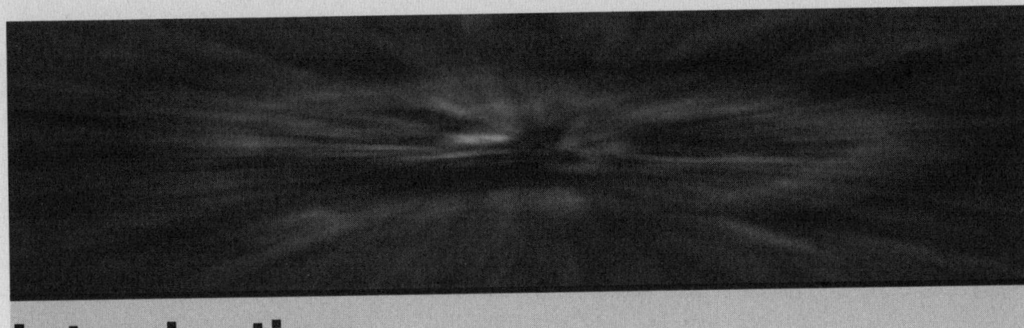

Introduction

READ THIS STUFF FIRST

Wouldn't it be great if all the problems on the verbal SAT looked like this:

10. PROPAGANDIZE : PRINCIPLES ::

(A) plagiarize : writing
(B) indemnify : damages
(C) indoctrinate : institutions
(D) pacify : aggression
(E) proselytize : religion* **(<—Hey you! Pick this one!)**

11. PALLIATE : WEIGHTY ::

(A)
(B)
(C) **This one's too hard. Just put down (B).**
(D) ***We* know you're smart—Love, ETS**
(E)

Only in our dreams is ETS (the company that writes the SAT) this benevolent. But believe it or not, the ETS test-writers *do* provide clues (sometimes on purpose, sometimes inadvertently) to every single question. This workbook will show you how to find those clues so that you can get every point you "deserve" on the verbal test—and maybe even a few that you don't.

In our section on sentence completions we'll show you how to spot the clues ETS has left for you. In our section on analogies we'll show you how to eliminate wrong answers—even when you don't know the meaning of the capitalized pair. In our section on critical reading, we'll show you how to find the important information in a passage—and skip the rest.

The techniques we'll be showing you are not just based on our opinions or private theories. They've been proven by more than 100,000 students who, over the past 12 years, have taken our SAT course.

But let's begin at the beginning.

What Is the Verbal SAT?

The verbal SAT is half of the SAT, a 3-hour multiple-choice test. The SAT contains three verbal sections, three math sections, and one experimental section that might be either math or verbal and does not count toward your score. The different sections do not come in any particular order, although math and verbal sections generally alternate. The three verbal sections consist of:

1. A 30-minute section made up of roughly
    - 9 sentence completions
    - 6 analogies
    - 15 critical reading questions based on 2 passages
2. A 36-minute section made up of roughly
    - 10 sentence completions
    - 13 analogies
    - 12 critical reading questions based on 1 passage
3. A 15-minute section made up of roughly
    - 13 critical reading questions based on 1 passage

How the Verbal SAT Is Scored

There are a total of 78 verbal questions on the SAT. Each correct answer earns you one "raw point." For each incorrect answer, ETS subtracts a quarter of a raw point. Your total raw score is then converted to a 200- to 800-point scale. Your verbal SAT score (along with your math SAT score) will be sent to you (and the colleges to which you are applying) about 5 weeks after you take the test. These scores are reported in 10-point increments. In other words, you can get a 510 or a 520, but never a 514. In practice, every 2 questions that you answer correctly will boost your verbal score by approximately 10 points on the 200-800 scale.

WHAT IS CONSIDERED A GOOD SCORE ON THE SAT?

The average verbal SAT score is approximately 500. If you want to find out what scores are required at particular colleges, you should consult one of the college guides found in bookstores (we are partial to *The Princeton Review Guide to the Best 345 Colleges*). Bear in mind that the colleges report either average or median scores, which means that many students with SAT scores well below the published average or median scores are accepted by those colleges.

In addition, colleges consider several factors when making admissions decisions. Your SAT score is a big factor, but not the only one.

HOW YOU TRULY SCORE HIGHER ON THE SAT

The real way to improve your SAT verbal score is to answer more questions correctly. We are going to be showing you many powerful techniques in this book, but let us begin by saying that the number one way to improve your score on the SAT is by improving your vocabulary. Nothing is more important—because the verbal SAT is simply a test of the words you know.

IMPROVING YOUR VOCABULARY

From a long-term perspective, a good vocabulary will win you good grades in college, jobs and promotions, and may even attract sophisticated and desirable members of whichever sex you find attractive.

And from a long-term perspective, the best way to build a better vocabulary is to read. A lot.

We heartily recommend this course of action, but we also recognize that if you have only one month until the SAT, there isn't time to read the collected works of Thackeray or even of Dave Barry.

However, from a short-term perspective, it turns out that learning a very small number of carefully selected words can really increase your verbal SAT score. We fed a computer all the words that have appeared on the SAT in the past 10 years; it has generated a list of roughly 250 words that appear on the verbal SAT with a regularity that is highly gratifying. These words (called the Hit Parade), along with the techniques for memorizing them, make up the bulk of the vocabulary section of this book. The words are arranged in small, useful groups, by situations.

At the back of the book, you will find detachable flash cards, each of which have Hit Parade words on one side and definitions on the other.

Before you go on, turn to our vocabulary section and think about a feasible schedule to memorize the Hit Parade words in the time remaining before you take the SAT. We promise you won't regret it.

Now let's talk strategy.

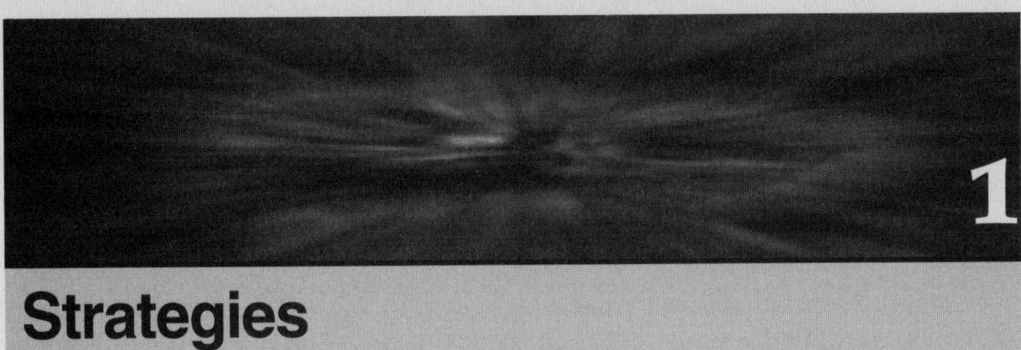

1 Strategies

THE ART OF ELIMINATION

Take a look at the following sentence completion—in an unusual format that you will never see on the SAT:

7. Bien qu'il soit trés vieux, il parait toujours _______.

You may think the unusual thing about this question is that it's in French, (okay, we admit that's pretty unusual), but the *really* unusual thing about this question—the thing that makes it different from every question on the verbal SAT—is that it's not in a multiple choice format.

You might be saying, "Who cares? Multiple choice or fill-in—I can't answer it anyway. It's in *French*."

As it stands right now, unless you speak French, you have no idea what word goes in the blank (and by the way, there are no questions in French on the SAT). But let's turn this question into a multiple-choice question—the only format you'll see on the verbal SAT—and see if you can figure out the answer now:

7. Bien qu'il soit trés vieux, il parait toujours _______.

   (A) earnest
   (B) timid
   (C) exhausted
   (D) jeune
   (E) elated

All of a sudden, this problem doesn't seem so hard, does it? Multiple-choice tests (in *any* language) always give test-takers an inherent advantage: there are only a finite number of possible choices. And while you might not know the correct answer to this problem, you know that four choices are probably wrong. (The correct answer is choice D.)

Eliminating Wrong Answers

There will be many problems on the SAT for which you will be able to identify the correct answer (particularly if you learn the Hit Parade words). However, there will be others about which you will not be sure. Should you simply skip these problems? The answer is: not if you can eliminate wrong answers. Wrong answers are often easier to spot than right answers. Sometimes they just sound weird. Other times they are logically impossible. While you will rarely be able to eliminate all the incorrect answer choices on an SAT question, it is often possible to eliminate two or three. And each time you eliminate an answer choice, your odds of guessing correctly get better.

Guessing Is Good

Every time you get a question right, ETS gives you one raw point. To discourage you from guessing at random, ETS deducts a quarter of a raw point from your score for each incorrect answer you choose. ETS calls this a guessing penalty, but in fact, it is not a penalty at all. Let's say you guess at random on five questions. The laws of probability say that you will get one of these questions right (so ETS gives you 1 raw point) and the other four wrong (so ETS takes away 4 quarter points). In other words, you will come out dead even. This means that guessing completely at random on the SAT won't help your score, and it won't hurt your score.

Ah, but who said anything about guessing at random?

Let's look at the same question again, but with slightly different answers:

7. Bien qu'il soit trés vieux, il parait toujours _______.

(A) earnest
(B) timid
(C) sérieux
(D) jeune
(E) elated

This time, even without knowing French, we can eliminate three of the answer choices. This gives us a fifty-fifty guess—much better than random guessing. It turns out that if you can eliminate even one answer choice, then it is in your interest to guess. You will find that our techniques in analogies and sentence completions will help you eliminate answer choices, even when you don't know the words.

ORDER OF DIFFICULTY

Analogy and sentence completion questions on the SAT are arranged in order of difficulty. For example, the 30-question verbal section always begins with nine sentence completions. These nine questions are arranged so that the easiest question comes first, the most difficult question comes last, and the others are arranged in ascending order of difficulty in between.

Following the sentence completions in the 30-question verbal section, there is a group of six analogies. The first analogy in the group is the easiest, the sixth is the most difficult, and the others are arranged in ascending order of difficulty in between.

The critical reading questions are *not* arranged in order of difficulty. Instead, these questions appear in the order in which the information that is required to answer them is found in the passage.

The difficulty level of a question reflects the percentage of test-takers who usually get that question correct. Depending on which words you happen to know, a question that is considered "hard" might be easy for you, while you might find an "easy" question to be difficult if it contains unfamiliar words. Nevertheless, it is a good idea to think of each group of questions in sentence completions and analogies as being in thirds. The first third is relatively easy. The second third is medium. The last third contains the questions that most people find difficult.

Easy Questions Have Easy Answers—Hard Questions Have Hard Answers

The order of difficulty is important because it will prevent you from overthinking. An easy question is supposed to have an easy answer. A difficult problem will have a difficult answer. If you find yourself wrestling with the first analogy, you are probably looking for subtlety that isn't there. If you find yourself picking the first choice that comes into your head on the last analogy, you may want to think it through again.

Verbal Distracters

The ETS test-writers think constantly about the order of difficulty because they are obsessed with making sure that students correctly answer only the questions that they "deserve to get right." The average test-taker is supposed to get all of the easy questions right, some of the medium questions right, and then get all of the difficult questions wrong.

There's only one potential problem here: what if the average test-taker were to guess correctly on a difficult question? The ETS test-writers hate this idea so much that in the difficult third of a group of questions they sometimes include distracter answers that are designed to trick the average test-taker.

JOE BLOGGS

Joe Bloggs is our name for the average test-taker. He's the guy who always writes down the first answer that comes into his head. Since the first answer that comes into his head is correct on easy questions, he gets all the easy questions correct. And since the first answer that comes into his head is *sometimes* correct on medium questions, he gets *some* of the medium questions correct. But the first answer that enters Joe's mind is always wrong on difficult questions, so Joe Bloggs gets all of the difficult questions wrong.

To make sure this remains true, the ETS test-writers will occasionally help Joe to make the *wrong* decision. Let's see how this works. Here's an analogy from the last and hardest third of a group of analogies.

14. DEPORT : COUNTRY ::

(A) renounce : belief
(B) betray : nation
(C) expel : school
(D) elect : government
(E) repeal : law

Don't Be Like Joe

We'll be covering how to do analogies in detail very shortly, so don't worry if you aren't sure of how to get the correct answer. For now, suffice it to say that the correct answer to this difficult question will mimic the *relationship* between the two capitalized words, rather than the *meaning* of either of these words. However, our friend Joe doesn't know that—and when he is lost, he will pick answers that simply remind him of the capitalized words. Do you see an answer that would appeal to Joe Bloggs?

If you said choice B or D, you're right on target. Joe might not know the meaning of the first capitalized word "deport" but he recognizes the second word "country." Joe likes to pick choices that he understands and that remind him of the capitalized words. So when he looks down at the answer choices, his eyes immediately fasten on choices B or D because the words "nation" and "government" remind him of "country." These choices feel good to Joe, but they are both the wrong answer. The correct answer is choice C.

Remember, the only time you need to look out for distracter answers is in the last third of a group of questions (the hardest questions in the set).

PACING

In each of the 30-minute sections, you will be answering three different kinds of questions: sentence completions, analogies, and critical reading questions. How many questions of each type should you be answering? No matter what score you're shooting for, you should answer *all* of the sentence completions and *all* of the analogies. As we've already said, even if you don't know several words in a question, it may still be possible to eliminate at least one answer choice—and in that case you should guess.

Your goal in the sentence completions and analogies sections is to answer each question in 40 to 45 seconds. Of course some questions will take much less time than that. Others will take much more time.

If you are shooting for a 290 or below, you only have to do half of the critical reading questions in the 30-question section; about half of the questions in the 15-minute, 13-question section; and none of the questions in the 35-question section.

If you are shooting for a 300 to 390, you only have to do half of the critical reading questions in the 30-question section; almost all of the critical reading questions in the 15-minute, 13-question section; and half of the critical reading questions in the 35-question section.

If you are shooting for a 400 to 490, you'll need to answer most of the critical reading questions in the 30-question section; almost all of the critical reading questions in the 15-minute, 13-question section; and all of the critical reading questions in the 35-question section.

If you are shooting for a 500 to 800, you have to answer everything.

What Kind of Raw Score Will Get Me a 400? A 500? A 600? A 700?

In order to get a 400 you need to get a raw score of about 20. There are many ways to get a 20. For example, you could answer 20 questions correctly and leave the rest blank. Or you could answer 30 questions, but get 8 wrong (remember, ETS subtracts a quarter point for each wrong answer). You get the idea.

To Get: (scaled score)	You Need: (raw points)	30-question section	35-question section	13-question section	Total Questions
300	6	4	4	0	8
350	11	6	6	2	14
400	18	9	9	4	22
450	27	14	14	6	34
500	35	19	19	7	45
550	44	23	23	9	55
600	54	27	31	10	68
650	62	All	All	All	78
700	68	All	All	All	78
750	72	All	All	All	78
800	76	All	All	All	78

ADDITIONAL PRACTICE

We've organized this book to get you up to speed on each of the question types while you learn some key vocabulary words as well. But to get the full benefit of our techniques, you will need to prove to yourself that they work on real ETS tests. We recommend a book called *10 Real SATs*, put out by the College Board. It contains 10 released SATs and can generally be found in bookstores.

We suggest that you do not buy any other preparation material. Unfortunately, many other books have problems that look like SAT problems, but are not at all SAT-like. It's important that you practice on questions that are designed just like the ones on the real test.

THE PRINCETON REVIEW

You may find that you want more than just this book and some practice tests. Some students find it hard to motivate themselves; others need a more thorough review of certain areas. If you are one of these people, you might consider taking The Princeton Review SAT course.

While this workbook contains many of the principles of our course, there is no way to put everything into a book. For example, you will not get the benefit of four diagnostic exams scored by computer with printouts of your relative strengths and weaknesses. You will not have highly trained teachers to explain our techniques and work with you one-on-one if you need it. You won't have the camaraderie that develops in small classes of motivated students scoring at exactly your level.

If you want more information about our courses, offered all around the United States and in several countries abroad, call us at 1-800-REVIEW6.

TAKING CHARGE

So much in life is outside of our control, and sometimes it's hard not to let ourselves get pushed around. The process of taking the SAT can sometimes feel like that. They tell you when to show up. They tell you where to sit. They tell you when to begin and when to stop. They even tell you the *number* of the pencil that you must bring with you.

In the face of all this control, it's easy to think that there is nothing you can do to take charge, but in fact NOTHING COULD BE FURTHER FROM THE TRUTH.

The way you take charge is by preparing ahead of time. By learning the strategies and techniques we're going to show you in the chapters ahead. By learning what is actually going to be on the test. By being aggressive, and by eliminating wrong answers.

And the most important way you can take charge is by keeping your sense of perspective. It's only a test.

2

Sentence Completions

SENTENCE COMPLETIONS

Each of the two 30-minute verbal sections of the SAT begins with a group of sentence completion questions. There are always either nine or ten sentence completions per section, arranged in order of difficulty. Because of the terrific elimination techniques we will be showing you below, you will probably be able to take a good guess on all of the sentence completions—even when you don't know the definitions of some of the words.

Let's begin by looking at an example of a sentence completion that unfortunately you will *never* see on the SAT:

1 Jane _______ the VCR.

(A) installed
(B) dropped
(C) programmed
(D) stole
(E) shot

Why won't you ever see this question on the SAT? Because, the way this sentence is written, *all* of the answer choices would be correct. What? You didn't think choice E could be right? Well, how about this:

2 After trying unsuccessfully to program it for three hours, Jane _______ the VCR.

(A) installed
(B) dropped
(C) programmed
(D) stole
(E) shot

To make sure that only one answer choice is correct per question, ETS always provides you with a clue (such as the one you just saw above) within the sentence itself. The clause "after trying unsuccessfully to program it for three hours..." gives away Jane's state of mind, and helps us to choose the correct answer. Let's look at the same sentence written several different ways. See if you can supply the missing word:

3 While trying to lift it, Jane _______ the VCR.

(A) installed
(B) dropped
(C) programmed
(D) stole
(E) shot

4 Because she wanted to tape a program when she wasn't home, Jane _______ the VCR.

(A) installed
(B) dropped
(C) programmed
(D) stole
(E) shot

5 After breaking into the house through the window, Jane _______ the VCR.

(A) installed
(B) dropped
(C) programmed
(D) stole
(E) shot

(answers: 2E, 3B, 4C, 5D)

Each of these sentences contained a clue that led you to the correct answer. While the real SAT sentence completion questions are a bit more difficult, the same principle always applies. The way to answer a sentence completion question is to look for the clue that *must* be there, in order for the question to have one answer that is better than the others. There are three kinds of clues:

THE CLUE

Take a look at the following two questions.

1 The woman told the man, "You're very _______."

(A) handsome
(B) sick
(C) smart
(D) foolish
(E) good

2 The doctor told the man, "You're very _______."

(A) handsome
(B) sick
(C) happy
(D) foolish
(E) good

Which of these two questions actually has a single correct answer, question 1 or 2?

If you said question 2, you're exactly right. In question 2, there's only one possible answer: choice B. The words are the clue. Every sentence completion has a the clue: a key word or phrase that tells you what kind of word you need to fill in the blank.

TIP: Always be on the look-out for the clue: the word or phrase that ETS gives you to help anticipate the word that will best fit in the blank.

Here's an example.

5 So _______ was the young boy's behavior that his teachers decided to give him a gold star.

(A) exemplary
(B) unruly
(C) arrogant
(D) radical
(E) imaginative

THE PRINCETON REVIEW METHOD

Cover up the answer choices. ETS wants several of these choices to appear likely if you haven't found **the clue**. For example, if you were to look straight at the answer choices in this question, your eye might be caught by choice B, "unruly," or choice C, "arrogant"—just because those are often words a teacher might use to describe a student's behavior.

TIP: Cover up the answer choices until you have found the clue in the sentence.

Look for the clue. Have you spotted it? In this case, the clue was in the very last words of the sentence: "gold star." If these teachers want to give a student a "gold star," what word would you use to describe his behavior? Try making up your own word to fit the blank. If you chose a word like "good" or "excellent" or "flawless" you were right on track.

STEP 3

Look at the answer choices and see which one comes closest to the word you think should go in the blank. Eliminate any that are definitely wrong. In this case, we can eliminate choices B and C because they are almost exactly the opposite of the word we were expecting to find. **Physically cross off these two choices**. Would "radical" behavior necessarily lead to a gold star? Not really, so we can cross off choice D as well.

STEP 4

If you still have choices left, guess among the remaining possibilities. In this example, we are down to choice A, "exemplary," and choice E, "imaginative." If you know the meaning of the word exemplary (one of the words on our Hit Parade) then your choice is easy. But let's say for a moment that you aren't sure. The first thing to do in this situation is not to panic—we are down to a fifty-fifty guess, which is already pretty good. Now, if we don't know the meaning of the word, of course we can't cross it off. So let's look instead at the other word. Do teachers reward imagination? They might. But do they reward imaginative *behavior*? What exactly would imaginative behavior look like? Mostly, teachers only like imagination when it is in a composition or a finger-painting. It might be a little threatening if it exhibited itself in *behavior*.

You're down to A and E. Guess. If you picked choice A, you are 10 points ahead. Exemplary means "ideal", or "worthy of imitation."

QUICK QUIZ #1

Begin by covering up the answer choices. Try to spot the clue, and come up with your own idea of what the missing word might be. Then go to the answer choices and eliminate wrong answers. Finally, pick the answer you think is correct.

1 By means of her _______ demeanor, Lucy Ortiz calmly worked her way up to the position of head salesperson at the chaotic brokerage house.

(A) cunning
(B) serene
(C) frenzied
(D) gullible
(E) unstable

2 Large facial features have often been the mark of successful people; many of our recent presidents have had _______ noses.

(A) insignificant
(B) typical
(C) unusual
(D) prominent
(E) subtle

3 Sightings of the tern, a small marsh bird once considered endangered, are becoming almost _______.

(A) commonplace
(B) erratic
(C) precarious
(D) virtuous
(E) uniform

4 Glaucoma, a serious eye ailment that can lead to blindness, is almost always _______, if it is caught in its early stages.

(A) fatal
(B) congenital
(C) unethical
(D) verifiable
(E) treatable

5 The consummate opera singer Kathleen Battle has long had the reputation for being a difficult, even _______, personality.

(A) entertaining
(B) malleable
(C) contentious
(D) deliberate
(E) bland

1	A	B	C	D	E
2	A	B	C	D	E
3	A	B	C	D	E
4	A	B	C	D	E
5	A	B	C	D	E

Answers and Explanations: Quick Quiz #1

1 *B* The clue here was the word "calmly." You might have been thrown off by the "chaotic" atmosphere at the brokerage house, and thought that Lucy must be pretty chaotic herself in order to fit in. However, the sentence makes clear that it was her calmness that allowed her to succeed in the hectic business. If you came up with a word like "evenness" or "placid" or "tranquil," you were right on the money.

Looking at the answer choices, we can eliminate everything but choice B, "serene."

2 *D* The clue in this sentence was the word "large" referring to the facial features of successful people. What kind of noses, then, according to this sentence, would we expect to find on our recent presidents? If you chose words like "huge" or "big" or "gigantic," you were right on the money.

Choice C was tempting, because a really large nose would be kind of unusual, but choice D was better because it clearly signified "large."

3 *A* The clue here was the phrase, "once considered endangered." If the bird was *once* considered endangered, then it isn't *now*. What word would describe sightings of this bird, which is no longer in danger of becoming extinct? If you chose a word like "mundane" or "everyday" or "routine," then you are doing just fine. Both choices B and C would be good possibilities if the bird were still endangered, but since it is not, we can eliminate them. Choice E might seem tempting at first, but the secondary definition of uniform (not what a boy scout wears) is "identical or alike." The best answer is "commonplace."

4 *E* Both choices A, "fatal," and B, "congenital" (meaning "from birth"), are often used to describe diseases, but neither is the right answer this time. The clue in this sentence is the phrase "if it is caught in its early stages." What word would you use to describe a disease discovered in its early stages? If you came up with "curable" or "correctable" or "relievable," you were right on track. The best answer here was choice E, "treatable."

5 *C* The clue in this sentence was the phrase, "a difficult, even _______ personality." Whenever you see this format: (a _______, even _______), the second word is almost always a more extreme version of the first word. (For example, "The weather was gray, even gloomy.") Therefore, what we are looking for in this sentence is a more extreme version of the word "difficult." If you came up with words like "troublesome" or "argumentative" you were right on the money. The best answer is choice C, "contentious" (meaning "quarrelsome.")

TRIGGER WORDS

Certain words reveal a lot about the structure of a sentence. We call these words "trigger words." Trigger words work with the clue to help you figure out the meaning of the word in the blank. Take a look at the following sentence:

You're beautiful, *but* you're . . .

What kind of word would go in the blank? Something negative, such as "rude" or "unpleasant."

The word "but" in the sentence above tells us all we have to know: whatever has been expressed in the first half of the sentence is about to be contradicted in the second half. Words like "but" are structural clues to the meaning of the sentence.

Here's a list of the trigger words that signal a contradiction:

but	however
although	even though
despite	though
rather	on the contrary
yet	in contrast

On the other hand, there are other words that signal that the second half of the sentence will continue in the *same* general direction as the first half. Here's an example:

You're beautiful, *and* you're very. . .

What kind of word go in this blank? Something positive, such as "smart" or "sweet."

The word "and" in the sentence above tells us what kind of word will go in the blank: Whatever thought has been expressed in the first half of the sentence (something positive) will be *continued* or amplified in the second half (something positive). Words like "and", when they appear in a sentence completion problem, are also structural clues to the meaning of the sentence.

Here's a list of the words that signal a continuation or an amplification of the direction in a sentence:

and	in fact
not only	but also
because	indeed, even

Always circle these trigger words whenever you see them. These words, along with the clue, will help you to figure out the meaning of the blank.

QUICK QUIZ #2

Begin by covering up the answer choices. Try to come up with the missing word using trigger words and the clue. Then go to the answer choices and eliminate wrong answers. Finally, pick the answer you think is correct.

1 Despite government efforts at population control, the number of people in China continues to _______ rapidly.

(A) decline
(B) increase
(C) fluctuate
(D) stabilize
(E) deploy

2 Archeologists believed until recently that the ancient Mayans lived exclusively in permanent settlements, but new evidence suggests that some of the Mayans made seasonal _______.

(A) migrations
(B) resolutions
(C) renunciations
(D) sanctions
(E) speculations

3 During the height of the civil war, the diplomatic efforts by Sweden to enforce a cease-fire were regarded by both sides not only with _______ but also with derision.

(A) delight
(B) reverence
(C) scorn
(D) vigor
(E) yearning

4 The museum has many fine paintings by Van Gogh, including his _______ and haunted self-portrait with the bandaged ear.

(A) tranquil
(B) haughty
(C) colorful
(D) repetitive
(E) anguished

5 Although many of the people at the party accepted John's account of the evening's events, Jason believed it to be _______.

(A) generous
(B) credible
(C) unusual
(D) inferior
(E) apocryphal

1	A	B	C	D	E
2	A	B	C	D	E
3	A	B	C	D	E
4	A	B	C	D	E
5	A	B	C	D	E

Answers and Explanations: Quick Quiz #2

1 *B* The trigger word in this sentence ("despite") tells us the second half of the sentence is going to contradict the first. Since the first half refers to population *control,* what do you think the number of people is going to continue to do? If you said "multiply" or "grow" you were exactly right. The correct answer is choice B.

2 *A* The trigger word ("but") tells us that the new evidence is going to contradict what archeologists believed until recently. The missing word should mean something like "trips" or "movements." The best answer is choice A.

3 *C* The construction "not only...but also..." means that the word in front of the "but also" must be similar to the word after the "but also." Thus, the missing word must resemble the word "derision." If you know the meaning of "derision" then the choice is fairly clear. However, let's say for a moment that you aren't sure. Have you at least got a feeling about the word? Does it sound positive or negative? If you said, "negative," you were exactly right. Which of the answer choices also sounded negative? The word that is most similar to "derision" (meaning "mockery") is choice C, "scorn."

4 *E* An "and" injected in between two adjectives usually means the two adjectives must be somewhat similar. In this case, we don't know the first word describing a painting by Van Gogh, but it must be similar to the second word, "haunted." Which choices can we eliminate? It's pretty easy to eliminate choices A, C, and D. "Haughty" (meaning "arrogant or condescending") doesn't exactly seem similar to "haunted." The correct answer is choice E.

5 *E* The trigger in this sentence was the word "although," which signaled that the second half of the sentence would contradict the first. In the first half, we are told that many people accepted John's story as true. In the second half, we are supposed to learn that Jason did not. If you had to choose a word for the blank, what would it be? If you chose a word like "a lie" then you were right on track. Let's go through the answer choices. If Jason believed John's story was A, "generous," would that contradict the general belief that his story was true? Not really. If Jason believed John's story was B, "credible" (meaning "believable"), would that contradict the general belief? Actually, just the reverse. If Jason believed John's story was C, "unusual," would that contradict the general belief? Maybe. Let's hold on to that one and look at the other two. If Jason believed John's story was D, "inferior," would that contradict the general belief? Maybe. Let's hold on to that one as well. If Jason believed John's story was E, "apocryphal" (meaning "fictional or made up"), would that contradict the general belief? You bet. The best answer to this fairly difficult problem is choice E.

DEGREE OF DIFFICULTY

Because all sentence completions are arranged in order of difficulty, you can frequently learn important things about a missing word simply by the question number, which tells you how hard the question is. The first three sentence completions in a group are supposed to be relatively easy. This means that the correct answer to one of these questions should be a relatively easy vocabulary word as well. The middle three or four sentence completions are supposed to be of medium difficulty. The correct answers to these questions will be words of medium difficulty. The last three sentence completions are supposed to be quite difficult. The correct answers to these questions will be quite tough vocabulary words, or medium words that have secondary meanings.

If you didn't know some of the words in a difficult sentence completion question, you might think that you would have to leave it blank—but that is not necessarily the case. Let's see how you could use order of difficulty to eliminate answer choices on the last three sentence completions. What follows are only the answer choices from one of the last three sentence completion questions of an actual SAT. Based on the fact that tough questions tend to have tough answers, which of these choices are *unlikely* to be the correct answer?

(A) cosmopolitan
(B) wavering
(C) plucky
(D) vindictive
(E) bellicose

Put it this way: which of these words would be familiar to just about anyone? "Cosmopolitan" is a fairly common word, as are "wavering" and "plucky." Therefore, if we were simply to guess the answer to this difficult sentence completion without the benefit of the sentence itself, we would be tempted to pick either D, "vindictive," or E, "bellicose." The correct answer to this real ETS question turns out to be choice E. Will this work every time? Of course not. This is merely a last-ditch guessing strategy if you don't understand enough of the sentence to be able to search for contextual clues.

TIP: Remember: The answers to difficult sentence completions tend to use difficult vocabulary words.

The real value of this strategy comes when you have already eliminated several answer choices by other means: you're down to two, and you can't figure out which one is the answer. If the question is one of the last three sentence completions, you should pick the answer choice containing the more difficult word.

QUICK QUIZ #3

Pretend that the following are answer choices for the last, and therefore hardest, sentence completions in a set of 10. As a last-ditch guessing strategy, eliminate answer choices that seem too easy to be the correct answer to difficult problems.

8
(A) supplied
(B) tainted
(C) betrayed
(D) corrected
(E) increased

9
(A) complexity
(B) uniqueness
(C) exorbitance
(D) paucity
(E) fragility

10
(A) **already eliminated**
(B) indifference. .legitimate
(C) **already eliminated**
(D) immunity. .hyperbolic
(E) **already eliminated**

8 ⊂A⊃ ⊂B⊃ ⊂C⊃ ⊂D⊃ ⊂E⊃
9 ⊂A⊃ ⊂B⊃ ⊂C⊃ ⊂D⊃ ⊂E⊃
10 ⊂A⊃ ⊂B⊃ ⊂C⊃ ⊂D⊃ ⊂E⊃

Answers and Explanations: Quick Quiz #3

8 Eliminate choices A, D, and E. The correct answer to this real ETS question is choice B.

9 Eliminate choices A and B. The correct answer to this real ETS question is choice D.

10 Imagine that you have already eliminated A, C, and E through context clues, but you can't decide between choices B and D. Do either of them seem too easy to be the answer to a tough question? Eliminate choice B. The correct answer to this real ETS question is choice D.

IS A MISSING WORD POSITIVE OR NEGATIVE?

While sometimes you may not be sure *exactly* what word would fit the blank, you may be able to get a feeling for whether the missing word should be generally positive or generally negative.

> **6** When Lattitia Douglas was _______ by the railroad company in 1903, it represented a personal victory for her.

While we may not know exactly what word ETS was going to choose for this blank, we can be pretty sure it was a positive word based on the clue ("a victory").

Just as important, when we look at the answer choices, we may not know the meaning of every word, but we may have a "feeling" about certain words even without knowing their exact definition. Here are the answer choices to this question:

(A) censured
(B) lauded
(C) rebuked
(D) rebutted
(E) undermined

As you go through the vocabulary sections of this book, you will probably be amazed at how often the words you've just learned come up on real SAT practice sections. Since we show you only words that appear again and again on the test, this is really not all that amazing. However, for every new word that you learn, there will be several whose meanings you haven't quite memorized yet—but that you have *seen* several times before.

NOTE: You can only decide that a word is negative or positive if you have seen it before.

These are the words you may be able to identify as positive or negative. By the way, we don't mean to suggest that you should try this technique with words you've never encountered before. Looking at a mystery word and saying, "Hmm, I don't like the look of that word," doesn't count. You have to have seen it before and have a vague sense of what it means.

You may not know the exact meaning of each of the words above (remember to look them up when you're done with this example—several are from our Hit Parade) but you may have a *feeling* about whether they are positive or negative.

As it turns out, "censured," "rebuked," "rebutted," and "undermined" are all negative words. Since we are looking for a generally positive word to fill the blank, we can eliminate all four of them—or as many of them as you have a negative feeling about. The correct answer is "lauded," which means "praised."

TWO-BLANK SENTENCE COMPLETION

About half of the sentence completions on the SAT contain two blanks instead of one. The same clues we've already discussed above are vital in answering these questions, but to use these clues effectively, it helps to concentrate on one blank at a time. Think about it this way: When you go to buy a new pair of shoes, you can eliminate pairs that don't fit after trying on just one. If the left shoe doesn't fit, you don't bother trying on the right shoe. So try one blank at a time. If the answer choice doesn't fit for that one blank, you can eliminate it. Which blank should you start with? Whichever you think is easiest. Try the following sentence:

5 Although the food at the restaurant was usually _______, the main course was _______ by an overabundance of salt.

(A) bland. .enhanced
(B) indifferent. .supplanted
(C) delectable. .marred
(D) distinguished. .elevated
(E) diverse. .superb

THE PRINCETON REVIEW METHOD

Cover the answer choices and read the entire sentence. Decide which blank you think would be easier for you to fill in with your own word. In this case, the first clause of the sentence, which contains the first blank ("Although the food at the restaurant was usually _______"), is not very helpful. The food might be delicious, or it might be terrible. We just don't know yet. Let's concentrate instead on the second clause of the sentence: "The main course was _______ by an overabundance of salt." How would you describe food to which much too much salt has been added? If you chose words like "ruined" or "spoiled" or "flawed," you were right on track.

TIP: In two-blank sentence completions, attack the blanks one at a time.

Completely ignoring the first word in each answer choice, take a look at the *second* word in each answer choice. We are looking for a word like "ruined." Clearly, choices A, "enhanced," D, "elevated," and E, "superb," are all wrong. Physically cross them off. Before we've even looked at the first blank, we're down to two possible choices!

Let's look at the first blank to decide between the two remianing choices. We've figured out that the second half of the sentence is saying that the food was bad. Did you notice that the first half of the sentence began with a trigger word? The word "although" told us that the second half of the sentence would contradict the first half. So let's summarize what we know about the sentence so far:

> Although the food at the restaurant was usually _______, tonight it was (something negative).

What kind of word are we looking for in the first blank? If you suggested "delicious" or "good" or "tasty," you were right on track. Let's look at the answer choices.

(A) **already eliminated**
(B) indifferent. .supplanted
(C) delectable. .marred
(D) **already eliminated**
(E) **already eliminated**

Remember that we have already crossed off three choices just by looking at the second blank. We're down to two remaining choices. Looking only at the first word in each, which do you think is closest to "delicious"? If you said choice C, you are 10 points ahead. "Delectable" means "highly pleasing." "Marred" (meaning "flawed") was much better than "supplanted" (meaning "to take the place of").

TWO-BLANK POSITIVE/NEGATIVE

On two-blank problems, you will sometimes need to watch out for the relationship between the two blanks. For instance, the blanks will often have a generally positive/generally negative relationship. Take a look at the question below:

> Although he was _______ by nature, his duties as a prison guard forced him to be more _______.

As always, we want to try to supply our own words before we look at the answer choices, but sometimes (as in this case) the sentence is a little too vague for us to supply precise words. Let's work with what we have. Did you notice the trigger word "although" at the beginning of the sentence? Because of this, we know that the first half of the sentence will contradict the second half. What kind of clues do we have in this sentence? In the second phrase, the sentence discusses how he must behave as a prison guard.

If you had to guess, do you think the second blank is going to be a generally positive word or a generally negative word? Even though we don't know exactly what the word will be, the second blank is likely to be negative. And *that* means that the first blank is likely to be positive.

Now let's look at the answer choices. It sometimes helps to actually write into the blanks the directions you think the words will go in, as shown:

6 Although he was (positive word) by nature, his duties as a prison guard forced him to be more (negative word).

(A) hermetic. .lonely
(B) lenient. .strict
(C) unhappy. .stylized
(D) gentle. .witty
(E) trite. .tactful

Even though we have a general idea of both blanks, it still makes sense to work on one at a time. We are looking for a generally negative word for the second blank. So let's eliminate any choices whose second words are positive. That gets rid of choices D, "witty," and E, "tactful." Cross them off with your pencil. Now let's look at the first blank in the answer choices that remain. The first blank should be generally positive, which means we can get rid of choices A, "hermetic," and C, "unhappy," as well. There's only one answer left: It must be choice B. Read the sentence again with "lenient" and "strict," just to make sure. Does one word contradict the other? Yes. Does the sentence make sense? You bet!

NEGATIVE/POSITIVE? POSITIVE/NEGATIVE? WHO KNOWS?

Probably the most difficult sentence completions are the ones in which all we know is the relationship between the blanks. Take a look at the following, and note the trigger word:

> Although he was _______ by nature, he has recently become more _______.

All that we really know about the missing two words in this sentence is that they must be opposites. Fortunately, problems like this appear infrequently on the SAT. When they do show up, you will be forced to go to the answer choices in search of opposites.

(A) generous. .frugal
(B) liberal. .dependable
(C) insensitive. .indifferent
(D) practical. .cooperative
(E) knowledgeable. .casual

Which pair of words above are opposites? The correct answer is choice A.

QUICK QUIZ #4

In each of the following sentences, try to decide whether the blanks should be positive or negative, or whether it is impossible to tell.

1 The new law will be very unpopular with the citizens of New Mexico because it _______ many _______ beliefs.

2 Despite the _______ of the men and women in the rescue team, their effort was _______.

3 The team had looked forward to the semi-final match with great _______, but the event proved to be_______.

4 Unlike their _______ ancestors, the whales of today are _______.

5 For all their apparent _______, the rich are just as _______ as the poor when it comes to an earthquake.

Answers and Explanations: Quick Quiz #4

1 – then +. The two words were "debunks" and "popular."

2 + then –. The two words were "courage" and "useless."

3 + then –. The two words were "enthusiasm" and "a debacle."

4 + then – or – then +. While we can't tell exactly what the values of the blanks are, we know they must be opposites. The two words were "solitary" and "gregarious."

5 + then –. The two words were "advantages" and "vulnerable."

GUESSING AND PACING

Even if you don't know some of the vocabulary words in a sentence completion, it is difficult to imagine a case in which you won't be able to eliminate at least one answer choice using the techniques we've just shown you. And if you eliminate one answer choice or more, then you *must* guess on the problem.

How long should you be spending on each group of 9 or 10 sentence completions? Six to seven minutes, if you plan to finish the verbal section. This works out to 40-45 seconds per problem. Of course, in the real world, you won't be spending exactly the same amount of time on each question; some will take 10 seconds, others will take much longer. Use the practice sections that follow to work on your pacing.

SENTENCE COMPLETION CHECKLIST

1. As you read the sentences, cover up the answer choices and look for:
    - The clue (meaning from the context of the sentence)
    - Trigger Words (_______ and _______ : two words are usually similar; _______ but _______ : two words are usually opposed)
    - Degree of Difficulty clues (easy questions have easy answers; hard questions have hard answers)
2. When there are two blanks, do them one at a time.
3. If you're having trouble with the meaning of the sentence or the individual words in the answer choices, think + or – .
4. Remember, it's often easier to eliminate wrong answer choices than to pick the right choice.

SENTENCE COMPLETIONS: PROBLEM SET 1

Each of the following sentences has one blank or two blanks, representing a word or words that have been left out of the sentence. Each set of answer choices contains a selection of words or sets of words that could be inserted into the blanks. Pick the answer choice whose word or words best completes the sentence.

Example:

State colleges do not accept students solely from within their states; on the contrary, they pride themselves on the _______ of their student bodies.

(A) popularity
(B) charity
(C) diversity
(D) indifference
(E) ingenuity
(answer: C)

Recommended time: 6 to 7 minutes

1 Though he claimed that the computer he had just purchased contained the latest features, in fact it was already _______.

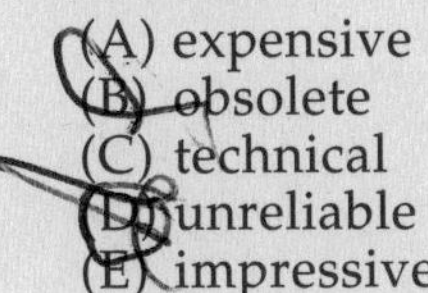

(A) expensive
(B) obsolete
(C) technical
(D) unreliable
(E) impressive

2 The city planner argued that the proposed convention center would create new traffic patterns, some of them benign, but others potentially _______.

(A) unexpected
(B) productive
(C) older
(D) harmful
(E) conventional

3 For most film audiences, the _______ of a scary event is more _______ than the event itself.

(A) anticipation. .frightening
(B) expectation. .skeptical
(C) experience. .mundane
(D) application. .interesting
(E) unfolding. .formal

4 It is unclear whether the new treatment will be approved for general use because its _______ has not yet been _______.

(A) usefulness. .denied
(B) diversity. .proven
(C) effectiveness. .established
(D) performance. .preserved
(E) integrity. .lampooned

5 Although Laura's uncle was _______ by nature, he was always _______ for his luncheon dates with his niece.

(A) predictable. .on time
(B) tardy. .punctual
(C) generous. .late
(D) unstable. .tardy
(E) hostile. .unprepared

6 Henrietta behaves in such _______ manner that no one expects her to accomplish anything.

(A) an intelligent
(B) a zealous
(C) a slothful
(D) an imperious
(E) an efficient

7 In their efforts to _______ the existence of a new strain of bacteria, scientists may be _______ by the lack of a suitable microscope.

(A) establish. .hampered
(B) eradicate. .aided
(C) disprove. .defined
(D) justify. .hindered
(E) substantiate. .unmoved

8 The young children who willingly stood on line for hours to get the basketball star's autograph, referred to him only in the most _______ terms.

(A) cynical
(B) detrimental
(C) neutral
(D) objective
(E) reverential

9 The doctor not only had _______ for the new treatment, but he also found it _______.

(A) a contempt. .necessary
(B) an esteem. .contagious
(C) a fondness. .irredeemable
(D) a disgust. .repugnant
(E) a weakness. .irrational

10 In her later paintings, the artist exchanged her wild brush strokes and chaotic layerings of paint for _______ attention to detail that verged on fussiness.

(A) a bohemian
(B) a fastidious
(C) an unconventional
(D) an indelible
(E) an opaque

1	A	B	C	D	E
2	A	B	C	D	E
3	A	B	C	D	E
4	A	B	C	D	E
5	A	B	C	D	E
6	A	B	C	D	E
7	A	B	C	D	E
8	A	B	C	D	E
9	A	B	C	D	E
10	A	B	C	D	E

WORDS YOU DIDN'T KNOW FROM PROBLEM SET 1

Before you check your answers below, take a minute to write down the words you didn't know from the previous questions. Look them up and review them tomorrow.

Word	Definition
______________	______________________
______________	______________________
______________	______________________
______________	______________________
______________	______________________
______________	______________________

Answers and Explanations: Problem Set 1

There are 10 sentence completions in this section, so we know that the first three will be relatively easy, the second four will be medium, the last three will be relatively difficult. Did you remember not to skip any questions?

1 *B* While most of the adjectives in the answer choices could describe a computer, the structure of the sentence provided a clue. The clue in this sentence was the phrase, "the latest features." However, the trigger word that began the sentence ("though") let us know that the second half of the sentence would be in opposition to the first. What would be the opposite of something that has all the latest features? That's right: obsolete.

2 *D* Again, the trigger word ("but") let us know that we were looking for a word that was in opposition to something that came before —but *which* something? If you picked choice C, you thought the missing word should oppose the "new" traffic patterns. However, in this sentence, the clue was the word "benign" and the "but" was contrasting two types of traffic patterns: "some of them benign...but others _______." Thus, we needed a word that means the opposite of "benign."

3 *A* The construction "...of a scary event is more ______ than the event itself," makes it likely that the second blank will just be another word for "scary."

4 *C* In order for the treatment to be approved, it will have to be shown to be effective. Therefore, the first blank has to be a positive word such as "effectiveness," and the second word should also be a positive word, such as "proven." In choice A, "usefulness" is positive, but "denied" is negative. In choice B, "diversity" is positive but it doesn't seem like a word that describes a positive attribute for a treatment. Choice C gives us two positive words. In choice D "performance" might be okay, but would "preserving" a treatment help to get it approved? Choice E also gives us a positive first word, but the second word, "lampooned," is negative.

5 *B* The trigger word ("although") tells us that the second word is going to be in opposition to the first word. In choices A and D, the two pairs of words are not in opposition to each other—rather the reverse. In choices C and E the two pairs of words are unrelated to each other. Only choice B provides opposites: a "tardy" person is unlikely to be "punctual."

6 *C* Because no one seems to expect Henrietta to accomplish anything, we have to assume that she is putting out some kind of *negative* attitude. Which answer choices are negative? C and D are both possibilities. If she were being "imperious," Henrietta would be arrogantly ordering people around, and she might actually get a lot done, so we can eliminate choice D. "Slothful" means lazy and sluggish.

7 *A* The best clues in this sentence are the three words "the lack of." It seems like "the lack of" a suitable microscope would be kind of a problem for a scientist. Thus, the second blank needs to be filled by a word like "hampered" or "hindered." To fill in the first blank, we need to consider what a bunch of scientists would want to do about the existence of a new strain of bacteria. Well, they might want to eradicate (or destroy) the bacteria, but they wouldn't want to eradicate the *existence* of the bacteria. Also, scientists wouldn't be "aided" by the lack of a microscope. They might want to do things like "disprove" or "substantiate" but they wouldn't be "defined" or "unmoved" by the lack of a microscope.

8 *E* If the children willingly stood in line for hours to get the star's autograph, that implies that they think well of him. Thus, we are looking for a positive word to fill in the blank. "Objective" might be considered a positive word, but it doesn't have the connotation of respect that the children seemed to be showing. The best answer is choice E.

9 *D* Unlike a simple trigger word, the construction "not only...but also..." implies two thoughts that are quite similar. Thus we are looking for either two positive words or two negative words.

This was a difficult question (number 9 out of 10) so we should be on the look-out for Joe Bloggs answers. Choice B, containing the word "contagious," might be very tempting to Joe because the stem sentence is about a doctor. We can eliminate it simply because Joe wants to pick it. Each of the other answer choices mixes a negative word with a positive word except for choice D.

10 *B* The clues here were that the artist *exchanged* wild and chaotic stuff for something else, presumably pretty different. What would be an adjective very different from "wild" and "chaotic" that would describe "...attention to detail that verged on fussiness"? If you were thinking words like "conservative" or "careful" you were right on track.

Let's look at the answer choices. "Bohemian" (meaning "setting social conventions aside") is clearly wrong, as is "unconventional." "Fastidious" (meaning "careful with details") seems pretty good. "Indelible" (meaning "incapable of being erased") and "opaque" (meaning "not transparent") are both artsy words and so might seem tempting in this sentence about an artist, but neither mean "careful." The correct answer is choice B.

SENTENCE COMPLETIONS: PROBLEM SET 2

Each of the following sentences has one blank or two blanks, representing a word or words that have been left out of the sentence. Each set of answer choices contains a selection of words or sets of words that could be inserted into the blanks. Pick the answer choice whose word or words best complete the sentence.

Example:

State colleges do not accept students solely from within their states; on the contrary, they pride themselves on the _______ of their student bodies.

(A) popularity
(B) charity
(C) diversity
(D) indifference
(E) ingenuity
(answer: C)

Recommended time: 6 to 7 minutes

1 The shark possesses _______ sense of smell; in experiments, a small quantity of blood released into the ocean has _______ sharks from as far away as three quarters of a mile.

(A) a cautious. .maimed
(B) a keen. .attracted
(C) a deficient. .enticed
(D) a negligent. .repelled
(E) a foul. .frightened

2 When the computer chip first became available, many companies were quick to _______ it, hoping to _______ this technological innovation.

(A) reject. .benefit from
(B) deflate. .succeed with
(C) deny. .participate in
(D) embrace. .profit from
(E) accept. .escape from

3 The witness accused the young man of breaking the window, but later _______ the accusation.

(A) recanted
(B) recounted
(C) predicted
(D) arranged
(E) supported

4 In his extraordinary _______ of the daily life of the early colonists, the historian captured the _______ hardships of the first winter.

(A) revelation. .tranquil
(B) evocation. .bleak
(C) premonition. .dreary
(D) exacerbation. .tacit
(E) celebration. .blithe

5 Character traits that are quickly learned in social settings can often be altered just as quickly; by contrast, _______ characteristics are more difficult to _______.

(A) credible. .respect
(B) trivial. .protect
(C) abrupt. .supply
(D) tasteless. .believe
(E) innate. .modify

6 Although the number of opening moves in the game of chess is not _______, there are more than enough to confuse the beginner.

(A) circumscribed
(B) measurable
(C) estimable
(D) familiar
(E) infinite

7 The Big Bang theory is regarded as the most likely explanation for the beginning of the universe, but a few scientists, who regard the theory as _______, continue to search for an _______.

(A) practical. .estimate
(B) proven. .objective
(C) implausible. .alternative
(D) controversial. .agenda
(E) comprehensive. .answer

8 The composer saw his latest composition not as _______ the music he had traditionally composed but rather as a _______ progression.

(A) a continuation of. .lurid
(B) an alternative to. .contradictory
(C) an affront to. .despotic
(D) a departure from. .logical
(E) an interpretation of. .reasonable

9 When choosing works of art, museum curators should base their selections not on the artist's current _______ but rather on the artist's _______ qualities, for the public can be very fickle.

(A) tableaus. .trivial
(B) standing. .capricious
(C) renown. .enduring
(D) aesthetics. .impudent
(E) philanthropy. .innocuous

1 ⊂A⊃ ⊂B⊃ ⊂C⊃ ⊂D⊃ ⊂E⊃
2 ⊂A⊃ ⊂B⊃ ⊂C⊃ ⊂D⊃ ⊂E⊃
3 ⊂A⊃ ⊂B⊃ ⊂C⊃ ⊂D⊃ ⊂E⊃
4 ⊂A⊃ ⊂B⊃ ⊂C⊃ ⊂D⊃ ⊂E⊃
5 ⊂A⊃ ⊂B⊃ ⊂C⊃ ⊂D⊃ ⊂E⊃
6 ⊂A⊃ ⊂B⊃ ⊂C⊃ ⊂D⊃ ⊂E⊃
7 ⊂A⊃ ⊂B⊃ ⊂C⊃ ⊂D⊃ ⊂E⊃
8 ⊂A⊃ ⊂B⊃ ⊂C⊃ ⊂D⊃ ⊂E⊃
9 ⊂A⊃ ⊂B⊃ ⊂C⊃ ⊂D⊃ ⊂E⊃

WORDS YOU DIDN'T KNOW FROM PROBLEM SET 2

Before you check your answers below, take a minute to write down the words you didn't know from the previous questions. Look them up and review them tomorrow.

Word	Definition
______________	________________________
______________	________________________
______________	________________________
______________	________________________
______________	________________________
______________	________________________
______________	________________________

Answers and Explanations: Problem Set 2

There are nine sentence completions in this section, so we know that the first three will be relatively easy, the second three will be medium, and the last three will be relatively difficult. Did you remember not to skip any questions?

1 *B* Let's attack the first blank first. If the shark has no sense of smell to speak of, then it would be neither attracted to nor repelled by the blood in the water; the shark simply wouldn't know the blood was there. Thus, we want a word that indicates the shark has a "good" sense of smell. Looking at the answer choices, we can eliminate choices C, "a deficient," and D, "a negligent." Can anyone have a "cautious" sense of smell? Not really. And just to check, even if the shark did have a cautious sense of smell, how would the smell of blood "maim" the shark? Eliminate choice A. A "foul" smell is certainly an expression we have heard, but a foul sense of smell? Not too likely. To check, would a shark be *frightened* by the smell of blood? Not the sharks we knew and loved in Jaws I and II. Eliminate choice E. If the shark's sense of smell was "keen," then it would be attracted to the blood. The correct answer is choice B.

2 *D* This was one of the infrequent sentence completions in which the sentence itself does not completely clue us in as to which words will best answer the question. For example, the sentence could use two positive words to read,

> ...many companies were quick to utilize it, hoping to succeed with this technological innovation.

Or it could use two negative words to read,

> ...many companies were quick to dismiss it, hoping to ignore this technological innovation.

Either of these would be fine. So what we have to do here is look at the answer choices for either two positive words or two negative words. Choice A is – then +, choice B is – then +, choice C is – then +, choice D is + then +, and choice E is + then –. The correct answer is choice D.

3 *A* The trigger word ("but") lets us know that the witness did something in the second half of the sentence that was somewhat contradictory to what he or she had done in the first half of the sentence—and the only thing the witness did in the *first* half was to accuse the young man. What would be contradictory to making an accusation? The correct answer is choice A.

4 *B* In this question, the second blank was probably easier to start with. "Hardships" is a negative sort of word, so we can expect that the adjective used to describe it will be negative as well. This allows us to eliminate choices A, "tranquil," D, "tacit" (meaning "implied, or not stated outright"), and E, "blithe" (meaning "joyous").

Choices B and C remain, so let's look now at the first blank. C, "premonition" (meaning "a feeling that something is about to happen"), is unlikely. How could a historian have a premonition about something that happened 200 years ago? The correct answer is choice B. An "evocation" means "a bringing forth."

5 *E* The trigger word ("by contrast") tells us that the first blank describes character traits that contradict the "quickly learned" character traits described at the beginning of the sentence. Which of the first words in the answer choices is a rough opposite of "quickly learned"? Choice E, "innate" (meaning "existing in a person since birth"), is the only one.

Let's suppose for a minute that we weren't sure of the meaning of "innate." We would now have to tackle the second blank. The first half of the sentence talks about traits that "can be altered...quickly." The second half, by contrast, talks about traits "that are harder to _______." What word do you think might fit in this blank? If you said "change" or "altered," you are right on the money. The correct answer is choice E.

6 *E* Here's a summary of this sentence using the trigger word:

> Although _______, there's more than enough.

If we were talking about money, we might say, "Although we don't have *all* the money in the world, there's more than enough for us." If we were talking about a Thanksgiving turkey, we might say, "It isn't the biggest turkey in the world, but it's more than enough for us."

If we are talking about the number of opening chess moves, we would say, "The number of moves isn't infinite, but it's more than enough to confuse us."

7 *C* The trigger word ("but") tells us that the "few scientists" don't completely agree with the Big Bang theory. Let's tackle the first blank. Which of the answer choices implies doubt about the theory? Both choices C and D imply doubt. Thus, we can eliminate choices A, B, and E. If you don't buy one theory, do you search for an alternative or an agenda? The correct answer is choice C.

8 *D* The trigger word here is "not as [one thing] but rather as [something else]." Thus, the second half of the sentence is likely to contradict the first half.

If you check the answer choices for the different possible first words, you will notice that they are all nouns: "a continuation," "an alternative." The construction "not as [one *thing*] but rather as [some*thing* else]" must always compare two nouns. The possible second words are all adjectives describing the noun "progression."

This means the first blank must be a noun that contradicts the noun "progression." We can rule out choice A, "a continuation," because it is almost a synonym. Choices C and E have nothing to do with contradicting a progression, so we can eliminate them as well.

Choices B and D both contradict the notion of a progression, so let's hold onto them.

Now let's look at the second blank in our two remaining choices. The second blank is an adjective describing "progression." Which makes more sense? A "logical" progression or a "contradictory" progression? The best answer is choice D.

9 *C* In this tough question, the trigger word ("but") was helpful, but only up to a point, because the vocabulary was difficult. The second blank was probably the best place to start. What kinds of qualities do you think ETS would want museum curators to look for in an artist? If you said "good" qualities, you were exactly right. Looking at the second words in the answer choices, can we eliminate any because they were not good? Yes, if we knew what they meant. Choice A, "trivial," choice B, "capricious" (meaning "impulsive, whimsical") and choice D, "impudent" (meaning "disrespectful or rude"), can all be crossed off. Choice C, "enduring," is good, so let's hold onto that. Choice E, "innocuous" (meaning "causing or intending little harm"), is mildly good, so let's not eliminate it either.

Now let's look at the first words in our two remaining choices. The word "renown" means "fame." The word "philanthropy" means "the practice of giving money or support to worthy causes." A philanthropic artist might be of help to a museum, but this sentence suggests the curator ignores philanthropy in favor of an artist who causes little harm. That doesn't sound right. The correct answer is choice C.

SENTENCE COMPLETION: PROBLEM SET 3

Each of the following sentences has one blank or two blanks, representing a word or words that have been left out of the sentence. Each set of answer choices contains a selection of words or sets of words that could be inserted into the blanks. Pick the answer choice whose word or words best completes the sentence.

Example:

State colleges do not accept students solely from within their states; on the contrary, they pride themselves on the _______ of their student bodies.

(A) popularity
(B) charity
(C) diversity
(D) indifference
(E) ingenuity
(answer: C)

Recommended time: 6 to 7 minutes

1 The association agreed to _______ one of its members when she was discovered to have _______ an infraction of the association rules.

(A) discipline. .prevented
(B) denounce. .impeded
(C) censure. .committed
(D) honor. .supported
(E) promote. .aided

2 While old books are often considered _______ by modern readers, librarians see them as historic documents that allow us to look back through time.

(A) reclusive
(B) fascinating
(C) detrimental
(D) relevant
(E) obsolete

3 The robin, a bird common to the northeast, is neither rare nor reclusive, but is as _______ and _______ a bird as you can find.

(A) wily. .tolerant
(B) amicable. .wary
(C) commonplace. .amiable
(D) vulnerable. .capable
(E) powerful. .fragile

4 The professor's lecturing style was certainly _______, but he told his students that in teaching such a complicated subject, clarity was more important than levity.

(A) scintillating
(B) unbiased
(C) monotonous
(D) arrogant
(E) stimulating

5 During a ten-year period, Napoleon conquered most of the Baltic States and _______ Spain as well.

(A) vanquished
(B) forfeited
(C) reiterated
(D) transcended
(E) refuted

6 Unlike the unequivocal accounts provided by eye-witnesses, the evidence provided by the flight recorder was more _______, leading to the development of several different theories to explain the crash.

(A) indisputable
(B) ambiguous
(C) lucid
(D) infallible
(E) theoretical

7 Engineers attribute the building's _______ during the earthquake, which destroyed more rigid structures, to the surprising _______ of its steel girders.

(A) obliteration. .strength
(B) damage. .weakness
(C) survival. .inadequacy
(D) endurance. .suppleness
(E) devastation. .inflexibility

8 By nature he was _______, generally limiting his comments to _______ remarks.

(A) reticent. .terse
(B) stoic. .superfluous
(C) trite. .concise
(D) verbose. .succinct
(E) arrogant. .self-effacing

9 For several months, the broker persuaded _______ tourists to invest in
_______ real estate ventures that quickly went bankrupt.

(A) resourceful. .urbane
(B) insolent. .dependable
(C) gullible. .spurious
(D) prescient. .fabricated
(E) omniscient. .meritorious

1	A	B	C	D	E
2	A	B	C	D	E
3	A	B	C	D	E
4	A	B	C	D	E
5	A	B	C	D	E
6	A	B	C	D	E
7	A	B	C	D	E
8	A	B	C	D	E
9	A	B	C	D	E

WORDS YOU DIDN'T KNOW FROM PROBLEM SET 3

Before you check your answers below, take a minute to write down the words you didn't know from the previous questions. Look them up and review them tomorrow.

Word	Definition
________________	____________________________
________________	____________________________
________________	____________________________
________________	____________________________
________________	____________________________
________________	____________________________

Answers and Explanations: Problem Set 3

There are nine sentence completions in this section, so we know that the first three will be relatively easy, the second three will be medium, and the last three will be relatively difficult. Did you remember not to skip any questions?

1 *C* If the association member took part in the infraction, then it seems almost certain that the association will punish her. While it was just possible that the sentence was going to go the other way— i.e., they were going to reward her for *discovering* the infraction— the first possibility was more likely. Look through the answer choices and pick the one that works. The answer is choice C.

2 *E* The trigger word "while" opposes librarians' views of old books and those of modern readers. How do you think librarians are likely to feel about old books? If you said, "positive," you are right on track. That means the modern readers will feel negative. This gets us down to A, C, or E. Choice E is the best answer.

3 *C* When ETS sets up pairs of words in opposition (trigger word: "but") as it does here, it helps to deal with the pairs in the correct order: the robin is not "rare" but _______; not "reclusive" but _______. Thus for the first blank we want a word that means "not rare." For the second blank we want a word that means "not reclusive." The correct answer is choice C.

4 *C* The second half of the sentence following the trigger word "but" tells us that the professor is clearer than he is funny. So his style is "not funny." Which of the answer choices is closest to "not funny"? That's right, the answer is choice C.

5 *A* The trigger wird "and" tells us that the two verbs of the sentence are going to be similar. Napoleon *conquered* the Baltic states and *conquered* Spain as well. So we need a word like "conquered." The correct answer is choice A.

6 *B* The trigger word "unlike" tells us that the recorder's evidence was the opposite of "unequivocal." If you knew what "unequivocal" meant, this was a great clue. But if you didn't, there was another clue later in the sentence: the evidence of the flight recorder lead to *several different* theories. What kind of evidence would lead to several different theories? "Indisputable" evidence? Not likely. "Ambiguous" evidence? That sounds correct! "Lucid" (meaning "clear") evidence? No. "Infallible" (meaning "unable to be proven wrong") evidence? No. "Theoretical" evidence? Maybe, but "ambiguous" is better. The correct answer is choice B. "Unequivocal" means "certain, not open to interpretation."

7 *D* The clue here was the phrase, ". . .which destroyed more rigid structures." Obviously, unlike other buildings that were more rigid, *this* building didn't fall down. Let's attack the first blank first. What word would you pick to describe this building's performance during the earthquake? If you were thinking of words like "survival" or "strength" then you were right on track.

We can eliminate any answers that suggest the building was destroyed: choices A, B, and E. We are left with choices C and D. Now let's look at the second blank. Do you think the building's survival hinged on the "inadequacy" of its girders or the "suppleness" (meaning "the ability to bend easily") of its girders? "Inadequacy" is certainly wrong, but at first, you might think "suppleness" sounded wrong too. The two contextual clues here were "...more *rigid* structures," and ". . .the *surprising* _______." Steel girders are not usually thought of as being "supple," which is why the word "surprising" is appropriate.

8 *A* What made this a difficult question was its lack of clues. Really, there was only one small clue: the word "limiting," and one small trigger word: the second half of the sentence was *not* going to contradict the first half—it was going to continue in the same direction. With these two clues noted, let's take a look at the answer choices.

If he was "reticent" (meaning "untalkative, shy"), would this person limit himself to "terse" (meaning "brief, free of extra words") remarks? Sure. Let's just check the other answer choices. If he was "stoic" (meaning "having great emotional control"), would he limit himself to "superfluous" (meaning "unnecessary") remarks? No. If he was "trite" (meaning "overused, lacking freshness"), would he limit himself to "concise" remarks? No. If he was "verbose" (meaning "talkative"), would he limit himself to "succinct" (meaning "concise") remarks? No. If he was "arrogant" (meaning "overconfident"), would he limit himself to "self-effacing" (meaning "putting yourself last") remarks? No way! The answer is choice A.

9 *C* The second blank was a good place to start because it is supposed to be an adjective describing real estate ventures "that quickly went bankrupt." This clue tells us that our second blank will not be a tremendously positive word. We can eliminate choices A, "urbane" (meaning "highly sophisticated"), B, "dependable," and E, "meritorious."

Now let's tackle the first word in our two remaining answer choices. What kind of tourists would invest in bad real estate? If you were thinking of words like "naive" or "trusting" or "stupid" you were right on track.

"Gullible" means "easily deceived." "Prescient" means "being able to see the future." The correct answer is choice C.

SENTENCE COMPLETION: PROBLEM SET 4

Each of the following sentences has one blank or two blanks, representing a word or words that have been left out of the sentence. Each set of answer choices contains a selection of words or sets of words that could be inserted into the blanks. Pick the answer choice whose word or words best completes the sentence.

Example:

State colleges do not accept students solely from within their states; on the contrary, they pride themselves on the _______ of their student bodies.

(A) popularity
(B) charity
(C) diversity
(D) indifference
(E) ingenuity
(answer: C)

Recommended time: 6 to 7 minutes

1 The orator was so _______ that even those who were not interested in the subject matter found themselves staying awake.

(A) tactful
(B) listless
(C) pious
(D) intriguing
(E) sullen

2 It was obvious from the concerned look on David's face that his spendthrift habits had placed him in a _______ financial situation.

(A) solvent
(B) solid
(C) global
(D) precarious
(E) benign

3 To make sure their _______ would be heard, the coal workers went on strike to protest the _______ lack of safety precautions in the mines.

(A) voices. .generous
(B) demands. .deplorable
(C) complaints. .uneventful
(D) neighbors. .dangerous
(E) case. .immaculate

4 Some crops do not need to be replanted every spring; a grape arbor, while initially requiring intensive _______, can produce _______ harvests for many years afterward without much work.

(A) suffering. .barren
(B) negotiation. .rich
(C) labor. .cooperative
(D) inertia. .forgotten
(E) toil. .abundant

5 In his review, Greenburg argues that the _______ nature of this artist's paintings _______ the artist's conviction that the twentieth century has spun wildly out of control.

(A) chaotic. .reflects
(B) controlled. .demonstrates
(C) disordered. .belies
(D) symmetrical. .interprets
(E) dangerous. .saps

6 Henry Kissinger argued that a successful diplomat must always remain something of a _______, which is why he counseled President Nixon, known for his tough stance on communism, to normalize relations with communist China.

(A) novice
(B) pioneer
(C) paradox
(D) raconteur
(E) sluggard

7 A recent barrage of media reports on the health benefits of physical activity has fostered a national _______ exercise, but new studies show surprisingly little _______ in the life-expectancy of people who exercise.

(A) preoccupation with. . improvement
(B) revulsion toward. .increase
(C) obsession with. .decline
(D) conception of. .speculation
(E) solution to. .reduction

8 Although the playwright Ben Johnson was not highly regarded by most Elizabethans of his day, a few scholars of that time _______ his work and _______ many of his plays.

(A) championed. .obliterated
(B) disparaged. .legitimized
(C) abetted. .destroyed
(D) revered. .preserved
(E) invoked. .undermined

9 Previous to the discovery of one intact ancient burial site in Central America, it had been thought that all of the Mayan tombs had been _______ by thieves.

(A) eradicated
(B) exacerbated
(C) prevaricated
(D) subordinated
(E) desecrated

10 Unfortunately, during the process of making a motion picture it sometimes happens that _______ revisions, poor casting decisions, and hasty compromises can be _______ the original intention of the authors.

(A) well-planned. .essential to
(B) ill-conceived. .detrimental to
(C) uncompromising. .divergent from
(D) meticulous. .injurious to
(E) distorted. .fundamental to

1 (A) (B) (C) (D) (E)
2 (A) (B) (C) (D) (E)
3 (A) (B) (C) (D) (E)
4 (A) (B) (C) (D) (E)
5 (A) (B) (C) (D) (E)
6 (A) (B) (C) (D) (E)
7 (A) (B) (C) (D) (E)
8 (A) (B) (C) (D) (E)
9 (A) (B) (C) (D) (E)
10 (A) (B) (C) (D) (E)

WORDS YOU DIDN'T KNOW FROM PROBLEM SET 4

Before you check your answers below, take a minute to write down the words you didn't know from the previous questions. Look them up and review them tomorrow.

Word	Definition
______________	______________________
______________	______________________
______________	______________________
______________	______________________
______________	______________________
______________	______________________

Answers and Explanations: Problem Set 4

There are 10 sentence completions in this section, so we know that the first three will be relatively easy, the second four will be medium, and the last three will be relatively difficult. Did you remember not to skip any questions?

1 *D* What kind of speaker would make people stay awake even when they were not interested in what he was talking about? An *intriguing* speaker.

2 *D* The clues here were the "concerned" look on David's face and the word "spendthrift" (meaning "one who spends extravagantly"). Clearly his financial position is not too good. Choice A, "solvent," in this case means "able to pay all debts," so that's wrong. Choice E, "benign," means "harmless." The correct answer is choice D, "precarious" (meaning "unstable, insecure").

3 *B* Most people would choose to tackle the first blank first, and they would probably guess that the first word would be something like "demands." Unfortunately, a quick look at the answer choices shows us that four of the five alternatives sound possible. Oh well. Let's try the second blank. Do you think the lack of safety precautions in a coal mine would be a good thing or a bad thing? Obviously, the adjective describing this lack is going to be a negative word. This enables us to eliminate everything but choices B and D. Looking now at the first word in the two choices that remain, it is easy to see that "neighbors" makes no real sense.

4 *E* The trigger word "while" combines with the clue ("without much work") to tell us that although at first a grape arbor requires _______, later it's pretty easy. If the word you were thinking of was "work" or "labor" you were on just the right track. Looking at the first words in the answer choices, there are two that seem possible: choices C and E. Now, let's look at the second blank. Do you think the harvests are going to be described with a positive adjective or a negative adjective? You got it! We are looking for a good adjective. "Abundant" fits the bill. "Cooperative" is neither good nor bad, and makes no real sense. The correct answer is choice E.

5 *A* It seems likely that the artist's conviction (that things are out of control) might have something to do with the art he or she produces. Choice A works on this level. Choice B does not, for a "controlled" painting style doesn't demonstrate a world gone out of control. Choice C doesn't either, for a "disordered" style would not "belie" (meaning "expose as false") a world gone out of control. In choice D, a "symmetrical" style would not "interpret" a world gone out of control. Why would a painter's style of painting "sap" (meaning "to drain away") his or her convictions? The best answer is choice A.

6 *C* Kissinger advises the President to do something that seems to contradict Nixon's normal behavior. Which of these words describes contradictory behavior? Choice C, "paradox" (meaning "something that seems to contradict itself"), is the best answer. A "raconteur" is a "skilled storyteller," and a sluggard is a "person lacking energy."

7 *A* The trigger word "but" tells us that the second part of the sentence is likely to somehow contradict the supposed health benefits of exercise. Let's attack the second blank first: ". . . new studies show surprisingly little _______ in the life-expectancy of people who exercise." Considering that the result is surprising, what do you think the word should be? If you said "rise" or "increase" you were right on target.

Let's look at the answer choices. C and E can be ruled out right away, because they are headed in the opposite direction. Choice D doesn't make a lot of sense.

Now let's look at the first words in our two remaining answer choices. Choice A, "preoccupation with," seems right. Choice B, "revulsion toward," might be all right if the structural clue "but" had not been there. The correct answer is choice A.

8 *D* The trigger word "although" tells us that, contrary to most Elizabethans, the scholars mentioned in the second half of the sentence *did* like Ben Johnson. In this sentence, either blank is fine to start with, and your choice will probably be determined by whether you knew more of the vocabulary words for the first blank or for the second.

Let's say for a second that you didn't know the meaning of a number of the possible words for either blank in the answer choices. Why not try the +/– technique? Here are the correct symbols for the missing words in the sentence and the answer choices:

...a few scholars of that time <u>+</u> his work and <u>+</u> many of his plays.

(A) + .. –
(B) – .. +
(C) + .. –
(D) + .. +
(E) ? .. –

Choice D was the only one in which both words were positive. "Revered" means "regarded with awe," "disparaged" means "spoke disrespectfully about," "abetted" means "acted as an accomplice or aided," and "championed" means "defended or supported."

9 *E* It's pretty clear from the context that we are looking for a word like "destroyed" here. Unfortunately, because this was the ninth question out of 10, the vocabulary is very tough. Even the negative/positive technique is not helpful here, because *all* the words are negative. The only real way to get this is to know the meaning of the correct word. "Desecrate" means "to abuse something sacred." "Exacerbate" means "to make something worse." "Prevaricate" means "to lie." "Subordinate" means "to place in a lower order." "Eradicate" means "to root out," which might have seemed tempting, but didn't give the sense of destruction of something sacred. The best answer is choice E.

10 *B* The first word of the sentence lets us know that the writer is not pleased with what is to follow. There is also a structural clue in the way the list of three things is presented in the middle of the sentence: _______ revisions, *poor* casting, *hasty* compromises. What word do you think belongs in the blank? That's right: something negative. Only two of the answer choices begin with negative words: B and E.

Now, let's look at the second blank. How do you think all these compromises and bad casting are going to affect the "original intention" of the authors? That's right—badly. Do we want "detrimental to" or "fundamental to?" The best answer is choice B.

SENTENCE COMPLETION: PROBLEM SET 5

Each of the following sentences has one blank or two blanks, representing a word or words that have been left out of the sentence. Each set of answer choices contains a selection of words or sets of words that could be inserted into the blanks. Pick the answer choice whose word or words best completes the sentence.

Example:

State colleges do not accept students solely from within their states; on the contrary, they pride themselves on the _______ of their student bodies.

(A) popularity
(B) charity
(C) diversity
(D) indifference
(E) ingenuity
(answer: C)

Recommended time: 6 to 7 minutes

1 The sculptor avoided the sharp angles and geometric shapes of abstract art, instead creating _______ shapes that seemed to expand or contract as one looked at them.

(A) static
(B) infallible
(C) fluid
(D) methodical
(E) residual

2 The initial _______ of many of the first-year law students _______ when they discover how many hours per week are necessary just to complete the course reading.

(A) apprehensiveness. .subsides
(B) torpor. .increases
(C) courage. .rebounds
(D) enthusiasm. .wanes
(E) satisfaction. .continues

3 The graduate student's radical theories were _______ by the elder scientist because they did not _______ the elder scientist's own findings.

(A) accepted. .confirm
(B) discounted. .corroborate
(C) confounded. .disprove
(D) praised. .prove
(E) tolerated. .support

4 Because the course was only an introduction to the fundamentals of biology, the students were surprised to be asked for such _______ information on the exam.

(A) irrelevant
(B) mundane
(C) redundant
(D) superficial
(E) esoteric

5 Torn between a vacation in Florida and a vacation in Wyoming, Lisa _______ for several weeks.

(A) vacillated
(B) mitigated
(C) terminated
(D) speculated
(E) repudiated

6 The lemur, a small monkey-like animal native to Madagascar, is not, as was once mistakenly thought, a direct _______ of man; new discoveries reveal that the lemur and man once shared a common ancestor but then proceeded on _______ evolutionary paths.

(A) relative. .converging
(B) ancestor. .divergent
(C) descendant. .synchronous
(D) terrestrial. .parallel
(E) subordinate. .similar

7 Although many believed that the problems of the community were _______, the members of the governing council refused to give in and came up with several _______ solutions.

(A) indomitable. .ingenious
(B) intractable. .inconsequential
(C) exorbitant. .promising
(D) irrelevant. .lofty
(E) obscure. .meager

8 No detail is too small for Coach Williams when her little league team is in a play-off game, but some parents find her to be too _______ and wish that she would spend more time _______ qualities such as good sportsmanship in her young charges.

(A) meticulous. .instilling
(B) circumstantial. .finding
(C) ambivalent. .impeding
(D) conspicuous. .obstructing
(E) ambidextrous. .thwarting

9 Despite _______ training, the new paratroopers awaited their first jump from an airplane with _______.

(A) paltry. .alarm
(B) comprehensive. .assurance
(C) extraneous. .indifference
(D) methodical. .presumptuousness
(E) extensive. .trepidation

1 ⊂A⊃ ⊂B⊃ ⊂C⊃ ⊂D⊃ ⊂E⊃
2 ⊂A⊃ ⊂B⊃ ⊂C⊃ ⊂D⊃ ⊂E⊃
3 ⊂A⊃ ⊂B⊃ ⊂C⊃ ⊂D⊃ ⊂E⊃
4 ⊂A⊃ ⊂B⊃ ⊂C⊃ ⊂D⊃ ⊂E⊃
5 ⊂A⊃ ⊂B⊃ ⊂C⊃ ⊂D⊃ ⊂E⊃
6 ⊂A⊃ ⊂B⊃ ⊂C⊃ ⊂D⊃ ⊂E⊃
7 ⊂A⊃ ⊂B⊃ ⊂C⊃ ⊂D⊃ ⊂E⊃
8 ⊂A⊃ ⊂B⊃ ⊂C⊃ ⊂D⊃ ⊂E⊃
9 ⊂A⊃ ⊂B⊃ ⊂C⊃ ⊂D⊃ ⊂E⊃

WORDS YOU DIDN'T KNOW FROM PROBLEM SET 5

Before you check your answers below, take a minute to write down the words you didn't know from the previous questions. Look them up and review them tomorrow.

Word	Definition
____________	____________________
____________	____________________
____________	____________________
____________	____________________
____________	____________________
____________	____________________

Answers and Explanations: Problem Set 5

There are nine sentence completions in this section, so we know that the first three will be relatively easy, the second three will be medium, and the last three will be relatively difficult. Did you remember not to skip any questions?

1 *C* This question would be more difficult if the wrong answer choices matched the level of difficulty of the right one. "Fluid" (meaning "capable of changing") is on our Hit Parade, and it's an important word to commit to memory.

2 *D* How would you feel if you had just gotten into law school—and you had really wanted to go there? Probably pretty good. Now, how would you feel if you found out that once you were there you were going to have to put in 50 hours per week just to keep up with the reading? Probably pretty bad. That is all you need to know to answer this question.

Initially they feel pretty [good], and then that good feeling [goes away]. If we start with the first blank, we can eliminate choices A, "apprehensiveness," and B, "torpor" (meaning "lack of energy").

Now let's look at the second words in the answer choices that remain. The only one that means "goes away" is D, "wanes" (meaning "to decrease in size").

3 *B* The elder scientist is either going to accept or reject the student's radical theories—so which one is it going to be? The clue here is ". . . the scientist's *own* findings." The scientist is only human; if the student agrees with the scientist, the scientist will be more likely to like the student. If the student *disagrees* with the scientist, the scientist will be more likely to throw out the student's wild theories.

Let's look at the answer choices. Choices A, D, and E make no sense because why should the scientist "accept," "praise," or "tolerate" theories that do not "confirm," "prove," or "support" his own? Choice B seems very likely because the scientist is "discounting" (meaning "to put a reduced value on, or to ignore") theories that don't corroborate his own. (By the way, if you got this one wrong, make a note to yourself to remember secondary meanings—"discounting" does not always have to take place in a store.) Choice C implies that the scientist disliked the ideas because they agreed with his own, which doesn't make sense. "Confound" means "to confuse or perplex."

4 *E* The trigger word "because" helps a little, but the key words here are "only" and "fundamentals." Here is a slightly simplified version of the sentence: "Because the course was really basic, the students freaked out at the [hard] questions on the test. We are looking for a word like "hard." The best answer is choice E, "esoteric" (meaning "known only by a select few").

5 *A* Basically, Lisa can't make up her mind. Which of these answer choices means that? Choice A, "vacillated," means "to go back and forth," and is the correct answer. To "mitigate" means "to make milder." To "repudiate" means "to disown, or refuse to acknowledge."

6 *B* Let's tackle the second blank first. The lemur and man once shared a common ancestor BUT (trigger word) they then. . .did something else. The "but" tells us that the sentence is going off in a different direction, just as apparently did the lemur and man. Which of the second words in the answer choices would indicate a new direction? There's really only one: choice B, "divergent." Just to check, let's look at the first blank now. In choice A, "relative" was possible, but "converging" (meaning "coming together") is the opposite of what we need. In choice C, "descendant" is wrong, because the monkey didn't evolve from man. Choice D doesn't make sense either because "terrestrial" simply means "living on the earth." In choice E, "subordinate," meaning "placed in a lower order," might be okay, but the two paths are *not* similar. The best answer is choice B.

7 *A* The first blank describes the community's problems, and the second blank describes the solutions. If we had to guess, the first word was going to be negative, and the second word was going to be positive. Let's tackle the first blank first. We need a negative word to describe problems. "Indomitable" (meaning "unable to be overcome") fits the bill, as does "intractable" (which means "not easily managed"). The other words don't really describe problems that the community refuses to give in about.

Now let's look at the second words in the answer choices that remain. "Ingenious" seems just right to describe solutions. "Inconsequential" (meaning "of little consequence, or importance") does not. The best answer is choice A.

8 *A* Let's look at the second blank. Parents think that qualities like good sportsmanship are important. Would they want the coach to "teach" these qualities in their children or "ignore" these qualities in their children? We want a word like "teach." Choices A and B provide words closest to "teach" for the second word. "Impeding," "obstructing," and "thwarting" are all negative words meaning "to prevent."

Now let's look at the first blank. The clue here is "No detail is too small" for the coach. However, note the trigger word "but" that follows. The parents think she is *too* detail-oriented. Which answer choice gives us a word like "detail-oriented" for the first blank? The best answer is choice A. "Meticulous" means "attentive to details." "Circumstantial" means "consisting only of details." "Ambidextrous" means "able to use either the right hand or the left hand equally well."

9 *E* This sentence could have gone one of two ways:

1) Despite (good) training, they awaited their jump with (fear), or 2) Despite (bad) training, they awaited their jump with (confidence).

Given the way most people feel about jumping out of an airplane, the first alternative seems more likely, and in fact, choice E gave us a clear version of that alternative. "Trepidation" means "fear." All of the other choices mixed up their meanings. For example, choice A said, roughly speaking, "Despite (bad) training, they awaited their jump with (fear)," and choice B said, roughly speaking, "Despite (good) training, they awaited their jump with (confidence)."

3

Analogies

ANALOGIES

Analogies follow directly after sentence completions in the two 30-minute verbal sections of the SAT. There will be a group of 6 analogies in one section and a group of 13 analogies in the other section. Each group of analogies is arranged in order of difficulty. Once you've learned the elimination techniques we will be showing you in this chapter, you will probably be able to eliminate at least one choice on every analogy—even when you don't know the definitions of some of the words.

Let's begin by looking at an example of an analogy that you will fortunately *never* see on the SAT:

POODLE : LAMPSHADE ::

(A) purse : laser
(B) mathematics : ocean
(C) love : encyclopedia
(D) suspenders : sword
(E) apple : psychologist

Why won't you ever see this question on the SAT? Because none of these words has *any* relation to any of the others. In order for an analogy to be an analogy, there has to be a direct relationship between the two words in the capitalized pair, and then that same relationship has to be mirrored in one of the answer choices.

What is the best way to figure out the relationship between the two words?

MAKE A DEFINITIONAL SENTENCE USING THE TWO WORDS

Let's say you are given WARDEN : PRISON. Saying "warden is to prison" may sound official, but it doesn't help you figure out the relationship between the two words. Instead, make a sentence that defines one word in terms of the other. In this case:

A *warden* is in charge of a *prison*.

As long as you can write a short sentence using one word to define the other, then there has to be a *clear and necessary* relationship.

A *captain* is in charge of a *ship*.

If the new pair of words fits perfectly into the same sentence, then the test-writers have found their analogy.

NOW CHECK THE REST

The best way to answer analogy questions on the SAT is to make a sentence that defines one word of the capitalized pair in terms of the other. Then go through the answer choices using the same sentence until you find a pair of words that fits the sentence exactly. Let's give it a try:

EAGLE : BIRD ::

(A) halibut : salmon
(B) beak : feather
(C) deer : fawn
(D) beagle : dog
(E) egg : chick

THE PRINCETON REVIEW METHOD

STEP 1

Make a sentence defining one of the capitalized words in terms of the other. A good sentence in this case would be, "An *eagle* is a type of *bird*."

Now try out the answer choices one at a time, putting the pairs of words into the same sentence, and see how they fit.

(A) "A *halibut* is a type of *salmon*." Is this true? Well, no, actually. A halibut and a salmon are two different kinds of fish. This answer choice is wrong. It's history. Throw it away.

(B) "A *beak* is a type of *feather*." Not possible.

(C) "A *deer* is a type of *fawn*." If these two words had been reversed, this answer choice *might* have been possible, but since they weren't, cross it off.

(D) "A *beagle* is a type of *dog*." Well, now we're getting somewhere. This seems like it must be right, but just to be sure you should always look at all the answer choices. ETS asks you for the "best" answer, and you won't know which one's best until you've seen them all.

(E) "An *egg* is a type of *chick*." Not really.

The best answer is choice D.

THE SIX INGREDIENTS FOR MAKING A GOOD SENTENCE

1. Make a Definitional Sentence

It isn't enough simply to make up a sentence with the two capitalized words in it. For example, here's a sentence that isn't going to do you much good:

> *Torpid* and *vigor* are two words I should seriously consider looking up real soon.

Instead, begin your sentence with one word followed by "is" or "means" then finish the sentence using the second word. Examples of good sentences are:

> *Torpid* means lacking energy, lethargic.
>
> A *torpid* person doesn't have much *vigor*.
>
> *Vigor* means something that has a lot of *energy*.

2. Keep the Sentence Short and Sweet

Make your definitional sentence as short as possible while still maintaining a proper relationship. And try to use an active verb as well. "A *suitcase* contains *clothes*" would be better than, "A *suitcase* has *clothes*."

3. Make Sure You Know What Parts of Speech Are Being Tested

Sometimes when you look at the capitalized pair of words in an analogy, you won't be sure whether they are nouns, verbs, or adjectives. Take a look at the following example:

WORRY : PANIC ::

(A) brain : intelligence
(B) happiness : bliss
(C) smile : anger
(D) agenda : list
(E) clock : time

Are *panic* and *worry* verbs or nouns? They could be either, of course, and in this case you really can't tell how they are being used just by looking at the capitalized pair of words. Fortunately, there's an easy way to figure this out. Look down at the answer choices. All five answer choices in an SAT analogy *must* offer the same two parts of speech as the capitalized pair—It's a rule. So if the answer choices are in the format noun : noun, then the capitalized words must also be noun : noun.

In this case, looking at answer choice A, we can tell immediately that both *worry* and *panic* are nouns, because *brain* and *intelligence* are both nouns.

A good sentence in this case would be "*Panic* is an advanced stage of *worry*," and the best answer is choice B: "*Bliss* is an advanced state of *happiness*."

Analogies can be in any of the following formats:

- noun : noun ::
- adjective : noun ::
- noun : verb ::
- verb : verb ::

Don't worry. We'll be showing you several examples of each. About half of all analogies are in the noun : noun :: format.

4. If You Reverse the Order of the Stem Words When You Make Your Sentence, Remember to Reverse the Words in the Answer Choices As Well.

You may have noticed that in that last example, the sentence we created ("*Panic* is an advanced stage of *worry*") used the capitalized words in the stem pair in reverse order. This is fine as long as you remember to reverse the words in the answer choices as well: "*Bliss* is an advanced state of *happiness*."

5. Make Your Sentence as Specific as Possible

Sometimes when you try putting the answer choices into your sentence, you will find that more than one answer choice fits your sentence. When this happens, simply make your sentence more specific. For example, try making a sentence for the analogy below:

BIRD : WINGS ::

(A) moose : antlers
(B) camel : hump
(B) spider : legs
(D) alligator : tail
(E) cat : whiskers

If your sentence for this analogy read, "A *bird* has *wings*," you were probably disappointed to find that *all* of the answer choices worked. A *moose* has *antlers*, a *camel* has a *hump*, a *spider* has *legs*, etc. To find the correct answer, we need to make the sentence more specific. How about this:

A *bird* is something that uses its *wings* to get around.

Now, if you try this sentence out with the words in the answer choices, only choice B works: A *spider* uses its *legs* to get around.

6. Be Willing to Be a Little Flexible

Every once in a while, the sentence you construct will work perfectly well with the capitalized words, but then will appear not to work with *any* of the answer choices. In this case, try rewriting your sentence slightly and see if that helps.

Don't be too concerned if your sentences don't exactly match the ones we come up with. For example, a few problems back we suggested the sentence "*Panic* is an advanced stage of *worry*." But if your sentence read,

"*Panic* is a really serious kind of worry,"

you probably got the same answer we did.

QUICK QUIZ #5

Using the guidelines we just discussed, construct a sentence for each of the following capitalized pairs of words, and check your sentence on the correct answer choice that follows. If you don't know a word, look it up. Hint: Some of these words are on our Hit Parade on Page 158.

1 MISER : MONEY ::

(A) squirrel : nuts

2 COUNSELOR : ADVICE ::

(D) donor : contribution

3 LEGIBLE : HANDWRITING ::

(B) lucid : thinking

4 SKEPTIC : DOUBT ::

(B) disciple : belief

5 BOTANIST : PLANTS ::

(C) ornithologist : birds

Answers and Explanations: Quick Quiz #5

1 "A *miser* hoards *money*," just as "A *squirrel* hoards *nuts*." Both of the capitalized words were nouns. If your sentence read "A miser has money," it probably would not have been specific enough to find the correct answer.

2 A good sentence would be, "A *counselor* is someone who gives *advice*." The correct answer, choice D, would read, "A *donor* is someone who gives a *contribution*." What if you wanted to say, "A *donor* <u>makes</u> a *contribution*," and thus thought choice D was wrong? If this happened, you would look at the other answer choices and, when you didn't find anything better, realize that you needed to be a bit flexible with your sentence in choice D.

3 "*Legible* means clear *handwriting*," would have been a good sentence, and choice B, the correct answer, would then read, "*Lucid* means clear *thinking*."

If your sentence had read, "*Legible handwriting* is easy to read," then you would have had to make a small leap to realize that choice B was correct: "*Lucid thinking* is easy to understand."

4 If you weren't sure whether *doubt* was a noun or a verb, look down at the second word in choice B. *Belief* is a noun. A good sentence for the capitalized pair would have been, "A *skeptic* is full of *doubt*," and the correct answer would have read, "A *disciple* is full of *belief*."

5 Even if you weren't quite sure what a *botanist* does, it was a pretty logical guess that "A *botanist* studies *plants*," just as "An *ornithologist* studies *birds*."

ETS'S FAVORITE ANALOGIES

It can be difficult to come up with good analogies, because not all words lend themselves to the format. This helps to explain why the same words repeat so often on the SAT (which is why it is so vital that you learn our Hit Parade—the Hit Parade words show up all the time). This is also why ETS has two favorite types of relationships:

1. Relationships of Degree
2. "Type of" or "Kind of" Relationships
3. "Lack of" or "Without" Relationships
4. "Is used to" or "Serves to" Relationships

1. Relationships of Degree

Think for a second about what sentence you would write for the following pair of words:

COLD : FREEZING ::

In a way, these words mean pretty much the same thing, but there is a slight difference—a difference of degree. Our sentence might read,

"*Freezing* means really <u>really</u> *cold*."

There are many pairs of words in the English language that denote differences of degree, and ETS has already found most of them and is looking for the rest. Whenever you do analogy problems, you can expect to run into one or two of them. Try the following Quick Quiz to see how they work.

TIP: Remember, if you reverse the order of the stem words when you make your sentence, always reverse the words in the answer choices as well.

QUICK QUIZ #6

Write a sentence for each of the following stem pairs (watching out for degree relationships) and then try out your sentence on each of the answer choices. Select the best answer. If you don't know a word, look it up and write it down in your vocabulary notebook.

1 PEBBLE : ROCK ::

(A) mountain : peak
(B) gravel : driveway
(C) sand : desert
(D) minnow : fish
(E) melon : fruit

2 LIVID : ANGRY ::

(A) vital : wary
(B) effusive : emotional:
(C) vain : beautiful
(D) resolute : weak
(E) old : modern

3 SAUNTER : WALK ::

(A) snore : sleep
(B) drawl : speak
(C) throw : toss
(D) ladle : brush
(E) finish : end

1 ⊂A⊃ ⊂B⊃ ⊂C⊃ ⊂D⊃ ⊂E⊃
2 ⊂A⊃ ⊂B⊃ ⊂C⊃ ⊂D⊃ ⊂E⊃
3 ⊂A⊃ ⊂B⊃ ⊂C⊃ ⊂D⊃ ⊂E⊃

Answers and Explanations: Quick Quiz #6

1 *D* If you didn't notice the degree relationship here, then you would probably have written a sentence like, "A *pebble* is a type of *rock*," in which case both choices D and E appeared to work.

A better sentence is, "A *pebble* is a small *rock*." Using this sentence, there is only one possible answer: choice D.

2 *B* A good sentence for the capitalized words would be, "*Livid* is very *angry*." You may not have known exactly what *effusive* meant in choice B, but you could be pretty sure none of the other answers was correct. Is *vital* very *wary*? Is *vain* very *beautiful*? Is *resolute* very *weak*? Is *old* very *modern*? The answer to all of these questions is no, and the best answer is choice B. (*Effusive* means "expressing unrestrained emotion.")

3 *B* A good sentence that expresses the degree relationship between the capitalized words is, "To *saunter* is to *walk* slowly." The best answer is choice B: "To *drawl* is to *speak* slowly."

---

2. "Type of" or "Kind of" Relationships

Here is another example of a common ETS relationship:

FLY : INSECT ::

What sentence would you use to connect these words? Something like:

"A *fly* is a type of *insect*."

or

"A *fly* is a kind of *insect*."

Try the following Quick Quiz for more examples of this kind of relationship.

QUICK QUIZ #7

Write a sentence for each of the following stem pairs (looking out for "type of" or "kind of" relationships) and then try out your sentence on each of the answer choices. Select the best answer.

1 ALLIGATOR : REPTILE ::

(A) fish : school
(B) lion : cat
(C) wolf : sheep
(D) cub : bear
(E) dog : bone

2 CHERRY : FRUIT ::

(A) flour : bread
(B) knife : utensil
(C) grass : water
(D) sail : ship
(E) leaf : tree

3 OXYGEN : GAS ::

(A) cobra : venom
(B) doctor : hospital
(C) aluminum : metal
(D) gymnasium : track
(E) airplane : cloud

Answers and Explanations: Quick Quiz #7

1 *B* A good sentence for the capitalized pair would be, "An *alligator* is a type of *reptile.*" Now, try the answer choices using the same sentence. Is a *fish* a kind of *school*? No. Is a *lion* a type of *cat*? Yes, so leave it in. Is a *wolf* a type of *sheep*? No. Is a *cub* a kind of *bear*? Maybe, so let's leave it in. Is a *dog* a type of *bone*? No. To decide between B and D, we need a more precise sentence. An alligator is a kind of reptile, just as a lion is a kind of cat, but a cub is a *baby* bear, not really a type of bear.

2 *B* A *cherry* is a type of *fruit*. What pair of words fits the same sentence? A *knife* is a type of *utensil.*

3 *C* *Oxygen* is a type of *gas*. Is a *cobra* a type of *venom*? No. Is a *doctor* a kind of *hospital*? No. Is *aluminum* a type of *metal*? Yes. Is a *gymnasium* a type of *track*? No. Is an *airplane* a type of *cloud*? No.

---

3. "Lack of" or "Without" Relationships

Another analogy relationship ETS loves to use is a capitalized pair in which one word means the lack of the other. What sentence would you write for the following pair of words:

EXHAUSTED : ENERGY ::

When you think about it, these words are almost, but not quite, opposites. Exhausted is not the opposite of energy, but rather:

"Exhausted is a lack of energy."

or

"Exhausted means to be without energy."

There are many pairs of words in the English language in which one word denotes the lack of the other, and ETS is fond of all of them. Whenever you do analogy problems, you can expect to run into one or two "lack of" or "without" relationships. Be on the lookout especially for words that begin with the prefixes *a* (as in "asexual"), *un* (as in "unethical"), or *in* (as in "indifference"), because these prefixes generally turn around the meaning of the word they are attached to. Try the following Quick Quiz to see how this all works.

QUICK QUIZ #8

Write a sentence for each of the following stem pairs (looking out for "lack of" or "without" relationships), and then try out your sentence on each of the answer choices. Select the best answer. If you don't know a word, look it up and write it down in your vocabulary notebook.

1 SHALLOW : DEPTH ::

(A) salty : ocean
(B) cloudy : height
(C) lurid : shock
(D) pious : faith
(E) apathetic : caring

2 BRAZEN : SHAME ::

(A) comprehensive : total
(B) inquisitive : curiosity
(C) moral : integrity
(D) oblivious : awareness
(E) witty : levity

3 AMORPHOUS : SHAPE ::

(A) morbid : death
(B) intrepid : fear
(C) fundamental : basics
(D) prominent : sight
(E) hopeless : pessimism

1 ⊂A⊃ ⊂B⊃ ⊂C⊃ ⊂D⊃ ⊂E⊃
2 ⊂A⊃ ⊂B⊃ ⊂C⊃ ⊂D⊃ ⊂E⊃
3 ⊂A⊃ ⊂B⊃ ⊂C⊃ ⊂D⊃ ⊂E⊃

Answers and Explanations: Quick Quiz #8

1 *E* A good sentence for the capitalized pair would be, "*Shallow* is a lack of *depth.*" Now, just go through the answer choices using the same sentence. Is *salty* a lack of *ocean*? No. Is *cloudy* a lack of *height*? No. Is *lurid* a lack of *shock*? Nope. Is *pious* a lack of *faith*? No. Is *apathetic* a lack of *caring*? Well, come to think of it, yes it is! The best answer is choice E.

2 *D* A good sentence for the capitalized pair would be, "*Brazen* behavior shows a lack of *shame.*" Now, just go through the answer choices using the same sentence. Does *comprehensive* behavior show a lack of *total*? No. Does *moral* behavior show a lack of *integrity*? Just the reverse. Does *oblivious* behavior show a lack of *awareness*? Well, if you know what *oblivious* means, you are probably saying, "This is our answer!" However, if you don't know the meaning of an answer choice, you can't cross it off. We'll hold on to choice D and come back. Does *witty* behavior show a lack of *levity*? Nope. The answer must be choice D. *Oblivious* does in fact mean "unaware."

3 *B* Even if you aren't sure of the meaning of "amorphous" (one of the words on our Hit Parade), it obviously must have some relation to shape, and you have one further clue—it begins with an *a*, which we know generally turns around the meaning of a word.

A good sentence for the capitalized pair would be, "*Amorphous* is a lack of *shape.*" Is *morbid* a lack of *death*? No. Is *intrepid* a lack of *fear*? Yes! (And by the way, did you notice the prefix "in"?) Let's look at the other choices just in case. Is *fundamental* a lack of *basics*? No. Is *prominent* a lack of *sight*? No. Is *hopeless* a lack of *pessimism*? No, no, no. The correct answer is choice B. "Amorphous" means "having no shape."

4. "Is Used to" or "Serves to" Relationships

The last of ETS's favorite relationships is the "Is used to" relationship. Here are a few examples:

OVEN : COOK ::

AX : CHOP ::

What kind of sentences would fit these pairs?

"An *oven* is used to *cook*."

and

"An *ax* is used to *chop*."

Look for these relationships in the next Quick Quiz.

QUICK QUIZ #9

Write a sentence for each of the following stem pairs (looking for "is used to" relationships), and then try out your sentence on each of the answer choices. Select the best answer. If you don't know a word, look it up and write it down in your vocabulary notebook.

1 SCISSORS : CUT ::

(A) window : close
(B) spice : season
(C) cloth : weave
(D) mask : frighten
(E) country : vote

2 GLUE : FASTEN ::

(A) laundry : fold
(B) bleach : color
(C) computer : repair
(D) steel : forge
(E) elevator : lift

3 ORNAMENT : EMBELLISH ::

(A) radio : repair
(B) antidote : poison
(C) detergent : clean
(D) carpenter : build
(E) rocket : launch

Answers and Explanations: Quick Quiz #9

1 *B* A good sentence for the capitalized pair would be, "Scissors are used to cut." Now let's see which choice best fits the sentence. Is a window used to close? No. Is a spice used to season? Yes. Is a cloth used to weave? No—a cloth is what gets woven. Is a mask used to frighten? Maybe, but that's not what the word "mask" means. Is a country used to vote? No. This makes B the best choice.

2 *E* What purpose does glue serve? "Glue is used to fasten." Likewise, "An elevator is used to lift."

3 *C* "An ornament is used to embellish." What choice matches this sentence? "Detergent is used to clean."

WHAT IF YOU DON'T KNOW A WORD IN THE CAPITALIZED PAIR?

You might think it would be impossible to answer an analogy question if you don't know one of the capitalized words, but there is a way.

Remember how ETS constructs an analogy. First, they come up with a pair of words that can be made into a short sentence, defining one word in terms of the other. Then they find another pair of words that fits exactly into that same sentence. This is their "best" answer. Then they write four other answer choices for camouflage.

The other four answer choices won't fit the sentence. In fact—here's the great part—some of them won't fit *any* sentence.

Frequently, several of ETS's camouflage answers contain words that aren't related to each other at all. And since, by definition, the correct answer to an analogy has to have a related pair of words, we can cross off any answer choice that doesn't.

To be the correct answer to an SAT analogy, a pair of words must have a definitional relationship. This means that you have to be able to define the meaning of one word in terms of the other.

Here are several real ETS analogy answer choices. See if you can make a sentence that defines one word in terms of the other:

wink : irritated

ambitious : activity

insincere : speaker

undress : coat

alibi : jury

It can't be done. The two words in each of these pairs are simply not related to each other. Now, you might argue that you can *always* write a sentence that manages to include *any* two words:

He *winked* at me, and I got really *irritated*.

But you can't write a sentence that defines one word *in terms of* the other, unless the two words are related to each other in the first place.

Here are several real ETS analogy answer choices that do have definitional relationships. Note how one word can be defined in terms of the other.

dog : kennel

composer : music

stingy : miser

QUICK QUIZ #10

In each of the following pairs of words, try to make a sentence defining one word in terms of another. If you can't, cross the pair off.

1 foot : shoe

2 throw : shoe

3 blush : embarrassed

4 incompetent : performer

5 incompetent : qualified

6 strand : hair

7 fragrant : blooming

8 fragrant : aroma

Answers and Explanations: Quick Quiz #10

1 A *shoe* protects a *foot*. You wear a *shoe* on your *foot*. Is there any way a dictionary could define shoe without using foot? Nope. This is a good relationship.

2 No relationship. Of course it's possible to throw a shoe, but you can't define *shoe* in terms of *throw*, or *throw* in terms of *shoe*. If this were an answer choice on an SAT analogy, you could cross it off.

3 "You *blush* when you're *embarrassed*." There might be some other reason to blush, but that's the big one, and this is a good relationship.

4 No relationship. If someone is *incompetent*, does that make him a *performer*? If someone is a *performer*, does that make her *incompetent*? No and No. Of course, you've probably heard these words used together from time to time (ETS likes to pick words that seem like they go together), but that doesn't mean that you can *define* one word in terms of another, and that's all that's important. If this were an answer choice on an SAT analogy (and it was), you could cross it off.

5 "An *incompetent* person is not *qualified*." Notice how this time, one of the words helps to define the other. This is a fine relationship.

6 "A *strand* is one piece of *hair*." This is a perfectly acceptable relationship.

7 A very weak relationship. If a flower is *blooming*, does that necessarily mean it's *fragrant*? Not all flowers have a smell. And besides, who said anything about flowers? A perfume can be fragrant, a pot roast can be fragrant, and neither of them have anything to do with blooming. If this were an answer choice on an SAT analogy (and it was), you could cross it off.

8 "Something *fragrant* has a nice *aroma*." Notice how in this case, we could define one of the words in terms of the other. This is a good relationship.

ELIMINATING UNRELATED PAIRS

We've already mentioned that analogies are arranged in order of difficulty. As you get to the second half of a group of analogies, you can expect to find words with which you are unfamiliar. If you don't know one of the capitalized words in an analogy, the first thing to do is go through the answer choices eliminating unrelated pairs. Crossing off wrong answer choices is a very effective way to find the right answer choice.

Let's say you don't know the definition of either of the two capitalized words in the following analogy (a safe bet, in this case). Are there any answer choices in this question that can be eliminated?

11 ☆✳✪✯✯✯✤ : ✯✧☆✪✱✯→★ ::

(A) occupation : success
(B) examination : room
(C) novice : experience
(D) oak : tree
(E) mayor : integrity

THE PRINCETON REVIEW METHOD

STEP 1

Ordinarily, we'd write a sentence with the capitalized words. But since we don't recognize them, we'll skip to Step 2.

Eliminate unrelated pairs.

(A) What would your sentence be? An *occupation* leads to *success*? Unfortunately, this is not necessarily true. Some occupations never lead to success, and success certainly doesn't always lead to an occupation. Cross off choice A.

(B) Is there a good relationship between *examination* and *room?* No way. Probably many *examinations* take place in a *room*, but you can't define either of these words in terms of the other. Eliminate.

(C) Well, we *can* write a sentence this time: "A *novice* has no *experience*." This appears to be one of those "lack of" relationships. Let's hold on to it.

(D) Is there a good relationship between *oak* and *tree*? Sure. "An *oak* is a kind of *tree*." We'll hold on to this one too.

(E) Is there a good relationship between *mayor* and *integrity*? Not necessarily. Some mayors have integrity, while others have gone to jail for their lack of integrity. Remember, if you can't come up with a sentence that defines one word in terms of the other, the two words aren't related. Cross it off.

We're left with two possibilities—a fifty-fifty guess. Not bad when you consider that we didn't know either of the capitalized words! (You'll find out what the missing words were as well as the answer to this question on page 83.)

ON THE SAT (UNLIKE LIFE) YOU DON'T HAVE TO WORK AT A GOOD RELATIONSHIP

You might argue in choice E above that if you just changed the sentence a little bit, it could have a good relationship. How about this: "In the best of all possible worlds, a *mayor* should be a symbol of *integrity*."

But the truth is, if you have to work this hard to find the relationship, it just isn't there.

If your sentence keeps getting longer and longer, with more and more conditions, then let it go—it's not your answer.

QUICK QUIZ #11

Eliminate the unrelated pairs from these medium-level analogies. Obviously, if you don't know a word in one of the choices, you can't eliminate that choice. Don't look up any words until after you've completed the drill.

1 ✳✪✭✫✭✤ : ✭✧✫✪✸✭→★ ::

(A) offensive : respond
(B) slippery : grasp
(C) lively : deliver
(D) discernible : see
(E) callous : soothe

2 ✳✪✭✫✭✤ : ✭✧✫✪✸✭→★ ::

(A) resign : employment
(B) dismiss : bonus
(C) inquire : curiosity
(D) close : window
(E) improve : renovate

3 ✳✪✭✫✭✤ : ✭✧✫✪✸✭→★ ::

(A) edit : manuscript
(B) ladle : soup
(C) steal : guilt
(D) inspect : funds
(E) spend : tax

4 ✳✪✭✫✭✤ : ✭✧✫✪✸✭→★ ::

(A) mellow : bright
(B) cautious : dangerous
(C) normal : deviant
(D) restrained : lazy
(E) daring : sad

Answers and Explanations: Quick Quiz #11

1 Choices A, C, and E can be crossed off. Each contains an unrelated pair of words. If something is *offensive*, do you necessarily *respond*? If something is *lively*, what does that have to do with *deliver*? If something is *callous* (meaning "hardened or cruel"), there is no necessary connection with *soothe*.

Of course, if you don't know the meaning of callous, then you will have to leave choice E in as a possibility.

Choices B and D had good relationships. Something *slippery* is difficult to *grasp*. Something *discernible* is easy to *see*. The missing words are PERPLEXING : COMPREHEND, and the correct answer is choice B.

2 Choices B and D can be crossed off because they contain unrelated words. To *dismiss* something or someone has nothing necessarily to do with a *bonus*. A *window* can be *closed*, but the fact that it can be closed is not one of its more important characteristics. Choices A, C, and E are all possible answers. The missing words are SCORN : CONTEMPT, about which you could have written this sentence: "To *scorn* something shows your *contempt* for it." The correct answer in this question is choice C: "To *inquire* about something shows your *curiosity* about it."

3 Choices C, D, and E all contain unrelated pairs and can be crossed off right away. Someone ought to feel *guilt* if he *steals*, but neither word helps to define the other. Similarly, there is no real connection between *inspect* and *funds*, or *spend* and *tax*.

Choices A and B are both possible. The missing words are RECTIFY : ERROR, which could fit the sentence, "To *rectify* is to correct an *error*." The best answer is choice A: "To *edit* is to correct a *manuscript*."

4 Choices A, D, and E all contain unrelated pairs. You can eliminate all of them. You might have thought that *mellow* had sort of a "lack of" relationship with *bright*, but in fact *mellow* is not considered the absence of *bright*. Being *restrained* has little to do with being *lazy*, and being *daring* has nothing to do with being *sad*. The missing words were SOUND : IMPAIRED. Your sentence might have been: "Something *impaired* is no longer *sound*." The correct answer is choice C: "Something *deviant* is no longer *normal*."

GUESSING

Eliminating unrelated answer choices will help you to answer analogy questions in which you couldn't make a sentence with the capitalized word-pair—but as you've just seen, it's rare to find an analogy where you can eliminate four unrelated pairs, leaving only the correct answer behind.

If you've gotten rid of two or three answer choices, and that's as far as you can go, then by all means guess between the remaining choices. As we said in the introduction, we make our course students guess on every single analogy. If you can eliminate even *one* answer choice, it's in your interest to guess. But before you do, consider one last important technique.

WORKING BACKWARD

We know that the two words in the correct answer choice ought to fit perfectly into a sentence constructed for the capitalized words. But isn't the reverse true as well? Shouldn't a sentence based on the two words in the correct answer make sense if you plug the capitalized words into it?

In other words, when you aren't sure of the meaning of the capitalized words, you can do analogies *backward*.

Here's how it works. Start with choice A. Decide if the two words are related by trying to make a sentence. If the words are unrelated, cross off choice A and move on. However, if you can make a successful sentence, then try that sentence out on the *capitalized* pair. If the capitalized words fit your sentence, you've found your answer. If they don't, go to choice B, construct a sentence, and repeat the process.

Now obviously if you had known the meaning of the capitalized words well enough to make a sentence in the first place, you wouldn't be working backward right now. On the other hand, you don't need to be nearly as clear about the meaning of two words to plug them into an already-constructed sentence.

Let's give it a try:

Remember we promised to show you the missing capitalized words to an analogy a few pages back? Here is that problem again:

11 PAUPER : WEALTH ::

(A) occupation : success—**already eliminated**
(B) examination : room—**already eliminated**
(C) novice : experience
(D) oak : tree
(E) mayor : integrity—**already eliminated**

THE PRINCETON REVIEW METHOD

Let's assume you are a little unsure about the meaning of *pauper*. We've already eliminated three answer choices because they contained unrelated pairs—so we're already down to a fifty-fifty guess, which is pretty terrific. But before we guess, let's try working backward.

The sentence we came up with for choice C was "A *novice* has no *experience*." Now let's try this sentence out on the *capitalized* pair of words. The idea is that even though we're not sure of the meaning of pauper, we may be able to tell if it sounds right in the sentence. Could a *pauper* have no *wealth*? This sounds possible.

The sentence we came up with for choice D was "An *oak* is a kind of *tree*." Could a *pauper* be a kind of *wealth*? This seems less likely.

The best answer is choice C. *Pauper* means "a very poor person."

DIFFICULT QUESTIONS HAVE DIFFICULT ANSWERS

In that last example, we were able to eliminate all four incorrect answer choices. Unfortunately, there will be times when this will not be the case. If you don't know more than one of the words, you'll probably only be able to eliminate two or three of the choices.

When all else fails, and you have to guess between two answer choices, there is one last method to make the choice slightly more scientific. As you know, the analogy questions are arranged in order of difficulty. Difficult questions have difficult answers. If you are stuck between two choices on a difficult analogy, the odds are slightly in favor of the more difficult word. For example, if you were stuck between the following two answer choices on an analogy in the last third of a section, which choice should you pick?

(A) newspaper : editor
(B) syllabus : instructor

Choice B contained the more difficult words, and thus was a better answer.

QUICK QUIZ #12

One of the capitalized words has been intentionally left out of each of these difficult-level problems to mimic what happens when you don't know the definition of a word. Go through the answer choices and try to decide if the words in an answer choice are related. If so, construct a sentence and work backward to see if your sentence seems to make sense with the capitalized word you have. Be sure to guess no matter how many or few of the choices you've been able to eliminate. Don't look up any words until after you've completed the drill.

1 ✯✫✦✪✤✯✦✯✦★ : FAVOR ::

(A) persecution : strive
(B) obsession : refuse
(C) money : swindle
(D) aversion : dislike
(E) stimulus : trust

2 RELIGION : ✯✫✦✪✯✪✦✯✪ ::

(A) freedom : sociologist
(B) art : artist
(C) surgery : administrator
(D) crime : culprit
(E) insects : entomologist

3 ✯✫✦✪✫✤ : ENERGY ::

(A) wry : behavior
(B) pensive : thoughts
(C) flat : contour
(D) profane : blasphemy
(E) dormant : entrance

1 ⊂A⊃ ⊂B⊃ ⊂C⊃ ⊂D⊃ ⊂E⊃
2 ⊂A⊃ ⊂B⊃ ⊂C⊃ ⊂D⊃ ⊂E⊃
3 ⊂A⊃ ⊂B⊃ ⊂C⊃ ⊂D⊃ ⊂E⊃

Answers and Explanations: Quick Quiz #12

1 *D* (A) There is no relation between *persecution* and *strive*. Eliminate.

(B) There is also no relation between *obsession* and *refuse*. Get rid of it.

(C) This is a good relationship. Your sentence might be, "To *swindle* someone is to take away his *money*." Now, let's work backward. Could "to *favor* someone" mean "to take away his _____"? What could you take away from someone that would favor him? This seems a bit unlikely, but let's hold on to it while we look at the other choices.

(D) This is also a good relationship. A good sentence might be, "To have an *aversion* to something means to *dislike* it strongly." Let's work backward: Could "to have a ______ for something" mean "to *favor* it strongly"? Sure.

(E) There is no relation between *stimulus* and *trust*. Eliminate.

We're down to choices C and D. Which one did you pick? The best answer is choice D.

The missing word is *penchant* (meaning "inclination, or bias toward"). To have a *penchant* for something means to *favor* it strongly.

2 *E* (A) There is no relationship between *freedom* and *sociologist*. Cross it off.

(B) A good sentence here would be, "An *artist* creates *art*." Now let's work backward: "A ______ creates *religion*." Is there a person who actually creates a religion? It doesn't seem too likely. Let's look at the other choices.

(C) There is no relationship between *surgery* and *administrator*. Eliminate.

(D) A good sentence here would be, "A *culprit* commits *crime*." Let's work backward: "A ______ commits religion." What type of person would commit religion? This seems highly doubtful. Let's keep looking.

(E) You may not be sure what an *entomologist* does—in which case you can't eliminate this choice.

If you don't know the meaning of *entomologist*, you are down to choices B (unlikely), D (highly doubtful), and E (unknown). So pick one. Don't soul-search. You might bear in mind that since this was a difficult question, the answer was likely to contain a difficult word. The best answer is choice E.

A good sentence for choice E would be "An *entomologist* studies *insects*." The missing word in the capitalized pair was *theologian*. "A *theologian* studies *religion*."

3 *C* (A) There is no relationship between *wry* (meaning "dryly humorous") and *behavior. Wry* is merely one kind of behavior out of hundreds. Cross it off.

(B) A good sentence here would be, "*Pensive* means full of *thoughts*." Let's work backward: "_______ means full of *energy*." This seems possible. Let's hold on to it and look at the other choices.

(C) A good sentence here would be, "Something *flat* is without *contour*." Working backward, could "something _______ be without *energy*?" This also seems possible.

(D) If you knew these two words, a good sentence would be, "Someone *profane* commits *blasphemy*." Could "Someone _______ commit *energy*?" This seems very unlikely because people seldom *commit* energy.

(E) There is no relationship between *dormant* (meaning "inactive") and *entrance*. Cross it off.

If you weren't able to make a sentence with choice D, then you eliminated it and you were down to choices B and C, a fifty-fifty bet. Both choices seemed possible. If you have no idea, just guess.

The missing word is *torpid* (meaning "without energy"). The best answer is choice C: "*Flat* is without *contour*."

JOE BLOGGS

On difficult analogies, Joe Bloggs can be counted on to choose the wrong answer. How does he do it?

Joe loves answer choices that remind him of the stem words. For example, if one of the stem words is *book*, when Joe sees the word *pages* in the answer choices, he immediately wants to pick it.

To make sure that Joe does not get any difficult analogies right by accident, the ETS test writers sometimes create distractor answer choices on difficult questions by creating answer choices that share the same subject matter as the stem words.

Here's a question from the last third of a group of analogies.

11 REPREHENSIBLE : CONDEMN ::

(A) torpid : rule
(B) innocent : judge
(C) depraved : admire
(D) estimable : praise
(E) worthy : parody

TIP: Remember, the only time you need to look out for Joe Bloggs answers is in the last third of a group of analogies.

Which of these answer choices would be tempting to Joe Bloggs? If you think Joe would choose B, you're exactly right. Joe might not know the meaning of the first capitalized word "reprehensible," but he recognizes the second word "condemn." Looking down at the answer choices, his eyes immediately fasten on choice B because the word "judge" reminds him of "condemn." So he picks it. And gets it wrong. The correct answer is choice D.

GUESSING AND PACING STRATEGIES FOR ANALOGIES

Even if you don't know some of the vocabulary words in an analogy, it is difficult to imagine a case in which you won't be able to eliminate at least one answer choice using the techniques we've just shown you. And if you eliminate one answer choice or more, then you must guess on the problem. No matter what score you are shooting for, please don't leave any analogy questions blank.

How long should you be spending on each group of 6 analogies? About 4 minutes. How long should you be spending on each group of 13 analogies? About 9 minutes. This works out to 40-45 seconds per problem. Of course, in the real world, you won't be spending exactly the same amount of time on each question; when you can make a sentence, you will sometimes have your answer in 15 seconds. When you have to work backward, this can take much longer. Use the practice sections that follow to work on your pacing.

ANALOGY CHECKLIST

1. Make a sentence with the capitalized words, and try the answer choices one at a time with the sentence until you find a match. To form a good sentence:
    - Know the meaning of the two capitalized words.
    - Use one word to define the other.
    - Keep the parts of speech consistent (noun : noun, noun : verb)

- If you reverse the order of the stem words when you make your sentence, remember to reverse the words in the answer choice as well.
- Make your sentence specific.
- Be flexible. You may have to rewrite your sentence a little.

2. Watch out for degree, "lack of," "type of," and "is used to" relationships.
3. If you don't know the meaning of the capitalized words, go straight to the answer choices. Try to construct a sentence using the pair of words in each answer choice. If the words aren't related, then the choice is wrong and can be eliminated. Remember, it's often easier to eliminate wrong answer choices than to pick the right choice.
4. If you can, construct a sentence based on the words in an answer choice, then try that sentence out on the *capitalized* pair to see if it seems to fit. This is called working backward.
5. Easy questions tend to have easy answers. Difficult questions tend to have difficult answers—with difficult vocabulary words.

ANALOGIES: PROBLEM SET 1

In each of the questions below you will find a related pair of words or phrases, followed by five more pairs of words or phrases. Choose the pair that most closely mirrors the relationship expressed in the original pair.

Example:

SMILE : HAPPINESS ::

(A) boredom : apathy
(B) cook : food
(C) comedy : laughter
(D) frown : anger
(E) resentment : mutiny

(answer: D)

Recommended time: about 4 minutes

1 FLOWERS : FLORIST ::

(A) rings : jeweler
(B) pharmacy : pharmacist
(C) roses : arrangement
(D) wedding : caterer
(E) stethoscope : doctor

2 HOARD : SAVE ::

(A) economize : spend
(B) revere : admire
(C) sulk : roar
(D) flirt : giggle
(E) ignore : notice

3 PLAYWRIGHT : ACTOR ::

(A) architect : custodian
(B) composer : musician
(C) biographer : celebrity
(D) soldier : colonel
(E) lawyer : judge

4 BUILDING : BLUEPRINT ::

(A) report : outline
(B) chicken : egg
(C) bricks : wall
(D) soup : ladle
(E) conduit : cement

5 ANTISEPTIC: GERMS ::

(A) sneezing : allergies
(B) earthquake : destruction
(C) water : thirst
(D) illness : fever
(E) executive : agenda

6 SLUGGISH : ENERGY ::

(A) sheer : cliff
(B) reticent : tact
(C) inebriated : memory
(D) trite : speech
(E) satiated : hunger

1 ⊂A⊃ ⊂B⊃ ⊂C⊃ ⊂D⊃ ⊂E⊃
2 ⊂A⊃ ⊂B⊃ ⊂C⊃ ⊂D⊃ ⊂E⊃
3 ⊂A⊃ ⊂B⊃ ⊂C⊃ ⊂D⊃ ⊂E⊃
4 ⊂A⊃ ⊂B⊃ ⊂C⊃ ⊂D⊃ ⊂E⊃
5 ⊂A⊃ ⊂B⊃ ⊂C⊃ ⊂D⊃ ⊂E⊃
6 ⊂A⊃ ⊂B⊃ ⊂C⊃ ⊂D⊃ ⊂E⊃

WORDS YOU DIDN'T KNOW FROM PROBLEM SET 1

Before you check your answers below, take a minute to write down the words you didn't know from the previous questions. Look them up and review them tomorrow.

Word	Definition
____________	____________________
____________	____________________
____________	____________________
____________	____________________
____________	____________________
____________	____________________

Answers and Explanations: Problem Set 1

There are six analogies in this section, so we know that the first two will be relatively easy, the second two medium, the last two relatively difficult. We hope you answered all six questions.

1 *A* A good sentence might be, "A *florist* sells *flowers*." The best answer is choice A: "A *jeweler* sells *rings*." A pharmacist *could* sell a pharmacy, but not every day. A caterer provides services for a wedding, but doesn't sell the wedding itself.

2 *B* This is a good example of degree relation: "To *hoard* is to *save*, only more so." The best answer is choice B: "To *revere* is to *admire*, only more so." Choices C and D do not have definitional relationships.

3 *B* A good sentence might read, "A *playwright* provides the material that an *actor* performs." The best answer is choice B: "A *composer* provides the material that a *musician* performs." Choice A, in addition to not fitting our sentence, does not have a definitional relationship.

4 *A* A good sentence might read, "A *blueprint* is the plan of a *building*." The best answer is choice A: "An *outline* is the plan of a *report*."

Let's say you started with a sentence like this: "A *blueprint* is the beginning of a *building*." In this case, two answers might seem possible: choices A and B. To decide among them, you would need to make your sentence a bit more specific: "A *blueprint* is the beginning (on paper) of a *building*."

Let's say you didn't know what a blueprint was. In that case, you could have worked backward from the answer choices. For example: "A *wall* can be constructed out of *bricks*, so can a *blueprint* be constructed out of a *building*?" That doesn't sound right.

A conduit (meaning a "pipe for carrying something") *might* be made of cement, but doesn't have to be. This is not a definitional relationship.

5 *C* A good sentence here would be, "An *antiseptic* helps eliminate *germs*." The best answer is choice C: "*Water* helps to eliminate *thirst*."

But what if you don't know what an antiseptic is? Then you work backward. There is really no relationship between *executive* and *agenda*, so we can cross off choice E right away. Let's make sentences with the remaining answer choices and check them against the original pair. *Sneezing* is sometimes caused by *allergies*. Is an *antiseptic* caused by *germs*? An *earthquake* causes *destruction*. Does an *antiseptic* cause *germs*? *Fever* is one sign of *illness*. Are germs a sign of *antiseptic*? Based on your responses to these questions, you can eliminate the choices you don't think are correct, and guess among the choices that remain. Choice A is very close to the original in subject matter, and on this difficult question, is probably a little too easy to be the correct answer. In other words, Joe Bloggs might have picked it.

6 *E* A good sentence would be, "*Sluggish* means without *energy*." The best answer is choice E: "*Satiated* means without *hunger*."

On a difficult question like this you're almost bound not to know some of the words. If you know the original pair, you can try the sentence you made with them on the other choices. For example, "*sheer* means without *cliff*." (This doesn't sound promising, does it?) Remember to look out for secondary meanings: Sheer, which usually means thin (as in sheer stockings), can also describe an almost vertical drop of a cliff-face. There is a *kind* of a relationship here, even if it is weak and not the right answer. If you know both words of any of the pairs in the answer choices, you can eliminate unrelated pairs. As it turns out, there is no relationship in choice B ("reticent" means "shy"—which has nothing to do with being tactful) or D ("trite" means "overused, or superficial"—which doesn't necessarily have anything to do with speech), and there is only a very weak relationship in choice C. ("Inebriated" means "drunk"—which might or might not affect a drunk's memory.)

ANALOGIES: PROBLEM SET 2

In each of the questions below you will find a related pair of words or phrases, followed by five more pairs of words or phrases. Choose the pair that most closely mirrors the relationship expressed in the original pair.

Example:

SMILE : HAPPINESS ::

(A) boredom : apathy
(B) cook : food
(C) comedy : laughter
(D) frown : anger
(E) resentment : mutiny
(answer: D)

Recommended time: about 9 minutes

1 LIBRARY : BOOK ::

(A) scholar : knowledge
(B) stable : horse
(C) factory : outlet
(D) laboratory : radiation
(E) laser : energy

2 MOVE : SCURRY ::

(A) scream : shout
(B) labor : rest
(C) breathe : pant
(D) arrest : indict
(E) jeer : mock

3 IRON : METAL ::

(A) hydrogen : water
(B) rock : quarry
(C) wheel : bicycle
(D) emerald : gem
(E) coral : ocean

4 EMIGRATE : COUNTRY ::

(A) retreat : position
(B) retire : pension
(C) voyage : suitcase
(D) swindle : property
(E) novel : old

5 INJURIOUS : HARM ::

(A) criminal : restitution
(B) insincere : dismay
(C) sacred : relic
(D) soporific : sleep
(E) unethical : principles

6 OMNIPOTENT : POWER ::

(A) impudent : control
(B) daring : audacity
(C) parochial : scope
(D) objective : rage
(E) beguiling : disgust

7 TEMPER : EXTREME ::

(A) deliver : speedy
(B) provoke : angry
(C) mitigate : severe
(D) slander : dishonest
(E) assuage : commodious

8 CARICATURE : DRAWING ::

(A) eagle : bird
(B) impersonation : flattery
(C) limerick : poem
(D) ballad : song
(E) license : hunter

9 INCORRIGIBLE : REFORMED ::

(A) unnerving : irritated
(B) innocuous : harmed
(C) irrelevant : verified
(D) insolvent : dissolved
(E) indelible : erased

10 PROPAGANDIZE : PRINCIPLES ::

(A) plagiarize : writing
(B) indemnify : damages
(C) indoctrinate : institutions
(D) pacify : aggression
(E) proselytize : religion

11 LOATHSOME : CONTEMPT ::

(A) strident : loneliness
(B) unwitting: awareness
(C) impudent : regret
(D) omniscient : understanding
(E) meritorious : esteem

12 NEOPHYTE : EXPERIENCED ::

(A) invalid : healthy
(B) pugilist : stubborn
(C) defendant : guilty
(D) scholar : erudite
(E) sentinel : guarded

13 HOSTILE : BELLICOSE ::

(A) indifferent : averse
(B) stubborn : obdurate
(C) morose : slothful
(D) unequivocal : skeptical
(E) angry: passive

1 ⊂A⊃ ⊂B⊃ ⊂C⊃ ⊂D⊃ ⊂E⊃
2 ⊂A⊃ ⊂B⊃ ⊂C⊃ ⊂D⊃ ⊂E⊃
3 ⊂A⊃ ⊂B⊃ ⊂C⊃ ⊂D⊃ ⊂E⊃
4 ⊂A⊃ ⊂B⊃ ⊂C⊃ ⊂D⊃ ⊂E⊃
5 ⊂A⊃ ⊂B⊃ ⊂C⊃ ⊂D⊃ ⊂E⊃
6 ⊂A⊃ ⊂B⊃ ⊂C⊃ ⊂D⊃ ⊂E⊃
7 ⊂A⊃ ⊂B⊃ ⊂C⊃ ⊂D⊃ ⊂E⊃
8 ⊂A⊃ ⊂B⊃ ⊂C⊃ ⊂D⊃ ⊂E⊃
9 ⊂A⊃ ⊂B⊃ ⊂C⊃ ⊂D⊃ ⊂E⊃
10 ⊂A⊃ ⊂B⊃ ⊂C⊃ ⊂D⊃ ⊂E⊃
11 ⊂A⊃ ⊂B⊃ ⊂C⊃ ⊂D⊃ ⊂E⊃
12 ⊂A⊃ ⊂B⊃ ⊂C⊃ ⊂D⊃ ⊂E⊃
13 ⊂A⊃ ⊂B⊃ ⊂C⊃ ⊂D⊃ ⊂E⊃

WORDS YOU DIDN'T KNOW FROM PROBLEM SET 2

Before you check your answers below, take a minute to write down the words you didn't know from the previous questions. Look them up and review them tomorrow.

Word	Definition
______________	________________________
______________	________________________
______________	________________________
______________	________________________
______________	________________________
______________	________________________

Answers and Explanations: Problem Set 2

There are 13 analogies in this section, so we know that the first four will be relatively easy, the second five medium, and the last four relatively difficult.

1 *B* If you tried the sentence, "A *book* can be found in a *library*," you were probably down to two choices: (A) "*knowledge* can be found in a *scholar*," and (B) "A *horse* can be found in a *stable*." Which is better? Try making a more specific sentence: "A *book* can be located in a *library*."

2 *C* A good sentence would be, "To *scurry* means to move *quickly*." The best answer is choice C: "To *pant* means to *breathe* quickly." None of the other choices defined one verb as a faster version of the other verb.

3 *D* The best sentence here would be, "*Iron* is a kind of *metal*," and the best answer is choice D, "An *emerald* is a kind of *gem*." Choices B and D both fit the same sentence "____ comes from _____." And choices A and C both fit another sentence, "_____ is a part of ______." If two of the answer choices fit the same sentence, then how could only one of them be correct? When you find two choices that fit the same sentence, you can eliminate both of them.

4 *A* "To *emigrate* means to leave a *country*," would be a good sentence, and the best answer was choice A, "To *retreat* means to leave a *position*." If you eliminated choice E because it had no relation, think again: *Novel* can also mean "new."

5 *D* A great sentence would be, "Something *injurious* causes *harm*." Even if you weren't sure of the meaning of *soporific*, you could still check the other answer choices by using the same sentence. Does something *insincere* cause *dismay*? Not necessarily. Does something *sacred* cause *relic*? Not really. Does something *unethical* cause *principles*? Nope. So could something *soporific* cause *sleep*? Sure. In fact, that's the exact definition of the word.

6 *B* A good sentence here would be, "*Omnipotent* means to have lots of *power*," but let's assume for a moment that your memory of omnipotent was a little hazy—in which case you couldn't make a sentence for the capitalized pair.

Should you then skip it? Of course not. First, let's eliminate any unrelated pairs and then we'll work backward. Eliminating unrelated pairs turns out to be very fruitful on this problem. Choices A, D, and E all contain relationships that are not definitional. For example, *beguiling* (meaning "charming") has only a very tenuous relation to *disgust*.

Let's look at our two remaining choices. *Parochial* means "having a narrow range," so a good sentence for the pair of words in choice C might have been, "Something that is *parochial* is narrow in *scope*." Does *omnipotent* mean something narrow in *power*?

Audacity means "bold or daring," so a good sentence for the pair in choice B might have been, "Someone who is *daring* has lots of *audacity*. Does *omnipotent* mean having lots of *power*? Well, yes, in fact, it does. "Omni" (meaning "all") in front of "potent" means something like "all potent."

7 *C* This is the seventh analogy, which means it's supposed to be of upper-medium difficulty. Therefore, *temper* probably won't mean the thing you lose when you're angry—there must be a secondary meaning. If you look at the answer choices for a moment, you'll get additional confirmation; the first word is a verb—to *deliver*.

A good sentence for the capitalized pair would be, "To *temper* means to make less *extreme*" and the best answer is choice C: "to *mitigate* means to make less *severe*."

If you didn't know the secondary meaning of *temper* ("to moderate") or the meaning of *mitigate* ("to make less severe") or *assuage* ("to soften or allay") you still could have eliminated choice A because the words did not have a definitional relationship, and choice D, which had a weak relationship.

8 *C* A good sentence for the capitalized pair might have been, "A *caricature* is an exaggerated *drawing*," and the best answer is choice C: "a *limerick* is an exaggerated *poem*." Choice B does not have a clear and necessary relationship. If you picked choice A, you probably made a sentence like, "A *caricature* is a type of *drawing*." This is not quite specific enough.

9 *E* "Someone who is *incorrigible* cannot be *reformed*," would be a fine sentence here—provided you knew the meaning of *incorrigible*.

Let's assume for a moment that you didn't.

First, eliminate unrelated pairs if there are any among the choices whose words you know. Choice A: "If something was *unnerving* (meaning "upsetting") it might make you *irritated*." This seems a little weak, but let's hold on to it while we look at the other choices. Choice B: It is difficult to make a sentence with *innocuous* (meaning "intending little harm") and the past tense *harmed*. There is really no relationship. Choice C: There is really no clear and necessary relationship here. Choice D: *Insolvent* (meaning "bankrupt") has nothing to do with the word *dissolve*, and hence, there is no relationship between *insolvent* and *dissolve*. Choice E: "Something *indelible* cannot be *erased*." This is a fine sentence. We're down between choice A, which is pretty weak, and choice E. Choice E is the best answer.

10 *E* A good sentence for the capitalized pair would be "To *propagandize* means to spread the word about one's *principles*."

Choice A: "To *plagiarize* means to copy someone else's *writing*."

Choice B: "To *indemnify* means to agree to pay for any *damages*."

Choice C: There is no clear relationship between *indoctrinate* (meaning "to instruct in a doctrine") and *institutions*.

Choice D: "To *pacify* means to remove *aggression*."

Choice E: "To *proselytize* means to spread the word about your *religion*." This is the best answer.

11 *E* A good sentence here might be, "Something *loathsome* deserves *contempt*." (*Loathsome* means "detestable.") If something is *strident* (meaning "harsh") does it deserve *loneliness*? No, so scratch choice A. Choice B is not a definitional relationship. If something is *unwitting* (meaning "unaware") does it deserve *awareness*? No, although this pair is at least related. If something is *impudent* does it deserve *regret*? Nope. If something is *omniscient* (meaning "all-knowing") does it deserve *understanding*? Not really. If something is *meritorious* does it deserve *esteem*? YES! Choice E is the best answer.

12 *A* A good sentence here would be, "A *neophyte* is not *experienced*," and the best answer was choice A: "An *invalid* is not *healthy*." If you didn't know the meaning of *neophyte* ("a beginner or novice") you still had several ways to get the right answer. For one thing, the root *neo* always means "new." A new anything is not likely to be experienced. This might have helped you come up with a sentence. If you didn't know *neo*, you could still have gone through the answer choices eliminating unrelated pairs. Is a *pugilist* (meaning "a boxer") someone who is *stubborn*? Not really. Is a *defendant* someone who is *guilty*? No. Is a *scholar* someone who is *erudite* (meaning "learned or scholarly")? Well, yes of course! Let's hold on to this one. Is a *sentinel* someone who is *guarded*? Well, a *sentinel* (meaning "a guard or watchman") might be *guarded* (the adjective *guarded* simply means "cautious"), but this relationship is a little weak.

We're down to A or E. Now, let's work backward. "A *scholar* is *erudite*." Is a *neophyte experienced*? "An *invalid* is not *healthy*." Is a *neophyte* not *experienced*? The correct answer is choice A.

13 *B* A good sentence for the capitalized pair would be, "*Bellicose* means very *hostile*." Knowing some of the common roots would have helped on this one: You might not have known exactly what *bellicose* meant, but you could have recognized it as coming from the same root as *belli*gerent and re*bell*ion.

Bellicose actually means "war-like" but let's again assume you didn't know that. To cross off some answer choices the first thing to do is eliminate any unrelated pairs. If you are *averse* to doing something, you are "disinclined" to do it—which is quite different from feeling *indifferent* about it. (If you're *indifferent*, you don't care one way or the other.) Thus, we can eliminate choice A. *Obdurate* means very *stubborn*, so choice B has a relationship, and we'd better hold on to it. *Morose* (meaning "gloomy," or "bad-tempered") has nothing to do with *slothful* (meaning "lazy") so we can eliminate choice C. *Unequivocal* (meaning "not ambiguous") has little to do with *skeptical*, so we can eliminate choice D as well. Is there a definitional relationship between *angry* and *passive*? Not really. Your behavior can be *passive* even if you're *angry*, and *passive* is not the lack of *anger* or vice versa. There is another reason not to pick choice E: Remember, a difficult question generally has a difficult answer. These are not only not difficult words, but *angry* is a little too close to *hostile* in the capitalized pair. This is probably a Joe Bloggs answer. The best answer is choice B.

ANALOGIES: PROBLEM SET 3

In each of the questions below you will find a related pair of words or phrases, followed by five more pairs of words or phrases. Choose the pair that most closely mirrors the relationship expressed in the original pair.

Example:

SMILE : HAPPINESS ::

(A) boredom : apathy
(B) cook : food
(C) comedy : laughter
(D) frown : anger
(E) resentment : mutiny

(answer: D)

Recommended time: about 4 minutes

1 BUS : PASSENGERS ::

(A) train : caboose
(B) car : tires
(C) freighter : cargo
(D) plane : pilot
(E) yacht : owner

2 GLAZE : POTTERY ::

(A) scuff : furniture
(B) donate : tree
(C) ice : cake
(D) injure : gun
(E) chortle : laugh

3 BURNISH : METAL ::

(A) cut : scissors
(B) deliver : box
(C) polish : wax
(D) sand : wood
(E) tarnish : silver

4 PROMONTORY : VIEW ::

(A) haven : refuge
(B) waterfall : revelation
(C) prison : interrogation
(D) church : diversity
(E) memorial : architecture

5 AMALGAM : METALS ::

(A) fracture : bones
(B) divorce : marriages
(C) coalition : factions
(D) car : payments
(E) convention : speeches

6 VERIFICATION : CONFIRM ::

(A) synopsis : avoid
(B) application : file
(C) obscenity: censor
(D) conciliation : appease
(E) reiteration : say

1 ⊂A⊃ ⊂B⊃ ⊂C⊃ ⊂D⊃ ⊂E⊃
2 ⊂A⊃ ⊂B⊃ ⊂C⊃ ⊂D⊃ ⊂E⊃
3 ⊂A⊃ ⊂B⊃ ⊂C⊃ ⊂D⊃ ⊂E⊃
4 ⊂A⊃ ⊂B⊃ ⊂C⊃ ⊂D⊃ ⊂E⊃
5 ⊂A⊃ ⊂B⊃ ⊂C⊃ ⊂D⊃ ⊂E⊃
6 ⊂A⊃ ⊂B⊃ ⊂C⊃ ⊂D⊃ ⊂E⊃

WORDS YOU DIDN'T KNOW FROM PROBLEM SET 3

Before you check your answers below, take a minute to write down the words you didn't know from the previous questions. Look them up and review them tomorrow.

Word	Definition
______________	________________________
______________	________________________
______________	________________________
______________	________________________
______________	________________________
______________	________________________

Answers and Explanations: Problem Set 3

There are six analogies in this section, so we know that the first two will be relatively easy, the second two medium, and the last two relatively difficult. We hope you remembered to answer all six questions.

1 *C* Your sentence might read, "A *bus* carries *passengers*." If you were feeling tempted by choices D or E, it would help to make the sentence a bit more specific: "The purpose of a *bus* is to carry *passengers*." The best answer is choice C.

2 *C* If you thought the first word in the capitalized pair was a noun, the answer choices should change your mind; the first word of each choice was a verb. A good sentence would be, "To *glaze* is to put a thin outer layer on *pottery*," and the best answer was choice C: "To *ice* is to put a thin outer layer on a *cake*." The pair of words in choice B was unrelated.

3 *D* Suppose you aren't sure what *burnish* means. Well, first of all, what part of speech is it? It has to be a verb, because all the answer choices start with a verb. Let's try an incomplete sentence: "To burnish is to (do *something*) to metal."

Choice A: "To *cut* is to (do something) to *scissors*." No.

Choice B: "To *deliver* is to (do something) to a *box*?" No.

Choice C: "To *polish* is to (do something) to *wax*?" No.

Choice D: "To *sand* is to (do something) to *wood*." Wait a minute. Yes, to *sand* is to smooth or polish *wood*.

Choice E: "To *tarnish* is to do something to *silver*." That sounds possible. To *tarnish* is to dull or discolor things, including *silver*.

Choices D and E are still in the running, so let's work backward. Could *burnish* be to smooth or polish *metal*? Sounds promising. Could *burnish* mean to dull or discolor *metal*? Maybe. You're down to fifty-fifty, so guess and move on. The correct answer is choice D.

4 *A* "A *promontory* is a place where you can find a *view*," is a good sentence for the capitalized pair of words, and the best answer is choice A: "A *haven* is a place where you can find a *refuge*." If you didn't know the meaning of *promontory* ("a high place, often jutting out into the water") you could have begun by eliminating unrelated pairs. The word-pairs in choices B, D, and E did not have clear relationships, and could be eliminated. Even the relationship in choice C was weak. An *interrogation* can take place in a *prison*, but it doesn't have to. Thus, you might have chosen choice A even without knowing one of the words in the capitalized pair.

5 *C* Let's say you didn't know the meaning of *amalgam*, and went straight to the answer choices. We could eliminate choices D and E because they don't have good relationships. Choices A and B both work with the same sentence: "A _____ is what happens when ______ break." ("A *fracture* is what happens when *bones* break." "A *divorce* is what happens when *marriages* break.") Since they can't both be right, we can eliminate them both. The correct answer is choice C: "A *coalition* is made up of different *factions*, just as an *amalgam* is made up of different *metals*."

6 *D* A good sentence here might have been, "*Verification* is the process by which you *confirm* something." The best answer is choice D: "*Conciliation* is the process by which you *appease* someone."

If you couldn't make a sentence with the capitalized pair, you could still have eliminated some unrelated pairs. In choice A, a *synopsis* (meaning "a plot summary") could be used as a way to *avoid* something (for example, you could use Cliff's Notes in order to avoid reading *Beowulf*), but a dictionary definition of "*synopsis*" would not use the word "avoid," and a dictionary definition of "avoid" would not use the word "synopsis." Really, when you think about it, these two words are not related. Similarly in choice B, *application* is not the process by which you *file* something. These words are not really related either.

You could then work backward from the remaining answer choices. A good sentence for choice C is, "*Censor* means to find and remove *obscenity*." Does *confirm* mean to find and remove *verification*? No. A good sentence for choice E would be, "*Reiteration* is the process by which you *say* something over again." Is *verification* the process by which you *confirm* something over again? Not really. That would be more like *re*verification.

Conciliation means "the act of winning someone over." To *appease* means "to pacify or conciliate."

ANALOGIES: PROBLEM SET 4

In each of the questions below you will find a related pair of words or phrases, followed by five more pairs of words or phrases. Choose the pair that most closely mirrors the relationship expressed in the original pair.

Example:

SMILE : HAPPINESS ::

(A) boredom : apathy
(B) cook : food
(C) comedy : laughter
(D) frown : anger
(E) resentment : mutiny
(answer: D)

Recommended time: about 9 minutes

1 MECHANIC : GARAGE ::

(A) artist : canvas
(B) administrator : personnel
(C) teller : window
(D) teacher : information
(E) nurse : hospital

2 SAP : TREE ::

(A) syrup : candy
(B) lint : clothes
(C) blood : mammal
(D) mold : bread
(E) fertilizer : plant

3 REPEAL : LAW ::

(A) withdraw : offer
(B) amend : agreement
(C) reconcile : amends
(D) demote : employee
(E) renovate : house

4 EPILOGUE : PLAY ::

(A) aria : opera
(B) trailer : movie
(C) afterword : book
(D) act : scene
(E) comedy : drama

5 TREASON : COUNTRY ::

(A) settlement : lawyer
(B) embezzlement : employer
(C) justice : honor
(D) hospitality : generosity
(E) chagrin : mistake

6 TERRITORY : DELEGATE ::

(A) whole : sample
(B) agent : manager
(C) lobbyist : senator
(D) pitch : salesman
(E) minority: majority

7 INQUISITORIAL : CURIOSITY ::

(A) morose : behavior
(B) injurious : prying
(C) ingenuous : innocence
(D) pernicious : damage
(E) laconic : speech

8 VULNERABLE : HURT ::

(A) fluid : changed
(B) vague: truncated
(C) virtuous : bribed
(D) witty : amused
(E) divergent : exploited

9 PREVARICATION : STATEMENT ::

(A) conflagration : fire
(B) preamble : introduction
(C) indifference : interest
(D) colt : horse
(E) pseudonym : name

10 ABBREVIATE : WORD ::

(A) laminate : layer
(B) inhibit : idea
(C) expedite : mail
(D) invoke : deity
(E) abridge : book

11 PATENT : OBVIOUS ::

(A) contrite : happy
(B) curt : expansive
(C) voracious : hungry
(D) dissonant : emotive
(E) ephemeral : exorbitant

12 MUNDANE : NOVEL ::

(A) rare : prevalent
(B) essential : imperative
(C) sealed : hermetic
(D) spontaneous : combustive
(E) judicious : minimal

13 CRITICIZE : CENSORIOUS ::

(A) explain : enigmatic
(B) discard : useless
(C) exude : flamboyant
(D) concur : sycophantic
(E) tremble : jocular

1	A	B	C	D	E
2	A	B	C	D	E
3	A	B	C	D	E
4	A	B	C	D	E
5	A	B	C	D	E
6	A	B	C	D	E
7	A	B	C	D	E
8	A	B	C	D	E
9	A	B	C	D	E
10	A	B	C	D	E
11	A	B	C	D	E
12	A	B	C	D	E
13	A	B	C	D	E

WORDS YOU DIDN'T KNOW FROM PROBLEM SET 4

Before you check your answers below, take a minute to write down the words you didn't know from the previous questions. Look them up and review them tomorrow.

Word	Definition
____________	__________________
____________	__________________
____________	__________________
____________	__________________
____________	__________________
____________	__________________

Answers and Explanations: Problem Set 4

There are 13 analogies in this section, so we know that the first four will be relatively easy, the second five medium, and the last four relatively difficult. Did you remember to answer all 13 questions?

1 *E* A good sentence for the capitalized pair is, "A *mechanic* works in a *garage*." The best answer is choice E: "A *nurse* works in a *hospital*." Choice C might seem tempting at first, but while a teller does work at a window, this is a bit too specific. Where is the window located? That's right—in a bank.

2 *C* If your sentence read, "*Sap* comes from a *tree*," you were left with two choices: B and C. To find the right answer, you had to make your sentence a bit more specific. "*Sap* is a liquid that circulates inside a *tree*," is a good sentence for the capitalized pair, and the best answer is choice C: "*Blood* is a liquid that circulates inside a *mammal*."

3 *A* You might have been tempted by choice B because it seems initially to have a very similar relationship to the capitalized pair. However, if you made a sentence, then you tossed out choice B right away: "To *repeal* means to take back a *law*." The best answer is choice A: "To *withdraw* means to take back an *offer*." If you *amend* an agreement, you change it, rather than take it back.

4 *C* A fine sentence would be, "An *epilogue* is the concluding part of a *play*," and the best answer is choice C: "An *afterword* is the concluding part of a *book*."

5 *B* "To commit *treason* is to betray your *country*," is a good sentence using the capitalized words. The best answer is choice B: "To commit *embezzlement* is to betray your *employer*." To *embezzle* means "to steal money by fraud."

6 *A* If you wondered at first whether there was a clear relationship between *territory* and *delegate*, we don't blame you—but remember, as far as ETS is concerned, there *has* to be a relationship between the two capitalized words. Your job is to find it. It helps to look at the answer choices and realize that the second word is a noun rather than a verb. What does a delegate do? She or he represents something or someone. Aha! "A *delegate* represents a *territory*."

Let's try this sentence out on the answer choices. Does a *sample* represent a *whole*? Actually, yes. We'll hold on to this while we check the other choices. Does a *manager* represent an *agent*? No. These words are not even related. Does a *senator* represent a *lobbyist*? We hope not. Does a *salesman* represent a *pitch*? No, he gives a pitch. Does a *minority* represent a *majority*? No. The best answer is choice A.

7 *C* A good sentence might read, "Someone who is *inquisitorial* has a great deal of *curiosity*."

Just for the sake of argument, let's assume that you don't know the meaning of *inquisitorial*, and therefore can't make a sentence. The first step? As always, eliminate unrelated pairs. Choice A can go because *morose* (meaning "gloomy") does not describe all *behavior*, and choice B is history because *prying* (meaning "peeping into someone else's affairs") is not necessarily *injurious*.

If you don't know the meaning of *ingenuous* ("naive and unsophisticated"), *pernicious* ("extremely harmful"), or *laconic* ("being of few words"), then this is as far as you can get on this problem. But don't leave it blank. Choose among choices C, D, and E. After all, one of them is right.

8 *A* A good sentence for the capitalized words would be, "*Vulnerable* means easily *hurt*."

We are now in the upper-middle of this section, and that means we have to look out for secondary meanings. For example, in choice A, you might have initially thought *fluid* was a noun meaning liquid. However, a quick look at the first capitalized word and the other answer choices will show you that the first word must be an adjective. Let's try our sentence: "*Fluid* means easily *changed*." Does that sound right? Well, we hope it does, since it's the right answer. Fluid means "changing readily, as a plan." To make sure, just try out the other answer choices in the same sentence.

(B) "*Vague* means easily *truncated* (meaning shortened)." That doesn't sound right.

(C) "*Virtuous* means easily *bribed*." No way.

(D) "*Witty* means easily *amused*." No.

(E) "*Divergent* (meaning "moving in a different direction") means easily *exploited*." No.

The best answer is choice A, even if you weren't sure of *fluid*'s secondary meaning.

9 *E* If you didn't know the meaning of *prevarication*, you had to work backward from the answer choices.

(A) "A *conflagration* is a really large *fire*." Is a *prevarication* a really large *statement*? That doesn't sound too likely.

(B) "A *preamble* is a short written *introduction*." Is a *prevarication* a short written *statement*? Maybe.

(C) "*Indifference* is a lack of *interest*." Is a *prevarication* a lack of a *statement*? Forget it.

(D) "A *colt* is a young *horse*." Is a prevarication a young statement? No way.

(E) "A *pseudonym* is a false *name*." Is a *prevarication* a false *statement*? Yes it is.

10 *E* A good sentence here would be, "*Abbreviate* means to shorten a *word*." You may not have known all the vocabulary words in the answer choices, but you probably knew enough to eliminate three unrelated pairs: Choices B, C, and D do not have good relationships. In choice A there is a relationship: "To *laminate* is to separate into *layers*"—but this did not fit the original sentence. Therefore it seems likely that the best answer is choice E. To *abridge* means to shorten a *book*.

11 *C* We're in the difficult part of the analogies section, so it wouldn't be likely that *patent* is the thing an inventor takes out to protect an invention—even if that had anything to do with the word *obvious*. Clearly, we are dealing with a secondary meaning here, but if you didn't know what it was, you still had options.

As always, you could go to the answer choices to eliminate unrelated pairs, and work backward. *Contrite* (meaning "deeply apologetic") has nothing to do with *happy*, so we can cross off choice A. *Expansive* (meaning "sweeping or generous") is sort of an opposite of *curt* (meaning "concise or brief"). Could *patent* mean not *obvious*? Maybe, so we'll hold on to choice B. *Voracious* means very *hungry*. Could *patent* mean very *obvious*? Maybe, so we'll hold on to choice C as well. *Dissonant* (meaning "unpleasant sounding") has nothing to do with *emotive* (meaning "showing emotion"), so we can cross off choice D. *Ephemeral* (meaning "short-lived or fleeting") has nothing to do with *exorbitant* (meaning "excessive"), so we can also cross off choice E.

It's either B or C. So pick one. *Patent* means very *obvious*.

12 *A* Again, we are dealing with a secondary definition of *novel*—not the noun-form meaning the book that you read, but the adjective-form meaning "new and different." *Mundane* means "ordinary or commonplace." A good sentence would be "Something that is *novel* is not *mundane*."

The vocabulary in the answer choices is quite difficult as well, so you may have limited success eliminating unrelated pairs or working backward. In choice A, something that is *prevalent* (meaning "in general use") is not *rare*. This was the right answer. In choice B, something that is *imperative* is *essential*. This is a good relationship, but the wrong sentence. In choice C, something that is *hermetic* is tightly *sealed*. Again, this is a good relationship, but it doesn't fit the original sentence. In choice D, ETS gives us two words that sometimes go together. Well, not everything that is *combustive* is *spontaneous*. This is an unrelated pair, and we can cross it off. There is also no clear relationship in choice E.

13 *D* If we knew what *censorious* meant, we could come up with this sentence: "A *censorious* person *criticizes* a lot." If we didn't know, we could at least eliminate choices C and E because they don't contain related pairs. Choice A contains a good relationship: "An *enigmatic* (meaning mysterious or puzzling) person doesn't *explain* much." Choice B contains a fair-to-poor relationship: "You tend to *discard* something if it is *useless*, although obviously, you don't have to." Choice D contains a good relationship: "A *sycophantic* (meaning flatteringly servile, saying yes to everything) person *concurs* (meaning "to agree") a lot."

ANALOGIES: PROBLEM SET 5

In each of the questions below you will find a related pair of words or phrases, followed by five more pairs of words or phrases. Choose the pair that most closely mirrors the relationship expressed in the original pair.

Example:

SMILE : HAPPINESS ::

(A) boredom : apathy
(B) cook : food
(C) comedy : laughter
(D) frown : anger
(E) resentment : mutiny
(answer: D)

Recommended time: about 9 minutes

1 LAME : MOBILITY ::

(A) lively : energy
(B) hostile : enemy
(C) hoarse : speech
(D) fractured : cast
(E) walk : transportation

2 BANKRUPTCY : MONEY ::

(A) discrepancy : account
(B) empathy : feeling
(C) plan : organization
(D) apathy : caring
(E) homely : household

3 ASTEROID : PLANET ::

(A) quibble : objection
(B) gravel : sand
(C) mountain : hill
(D) wood : splinter
(E) radio : television

4 EMBARGO : TRADE ::

(A) umbrella : clouds
(B) engine : automobile
(C) license : fishing
(D) alarm : valuables
(E) helmet : injury

5 ALTERATION : SUIT ::

(A) digestion : snack
(B) revision : story
(C) irrigation : crop
(D) cooking : apron
(E) detection : gun

6 RESOLUTE : DETERMINATION ::

(A) pristine : grace
(B) skeptical : doubt
(C) tainted : honor
(D) stringent : suggestions
(E) wary : risks

7 INAUDIBLE : AMPLIFIER ::

(A) incomprehensible : story
(B) imperceptible : microscope
(C) inadvertent : telescope
(D) heat : radiator
(E) unknown : mystery

8 VACILLATE : INDECISION ::

(A) lament : woe
(B) hibernate : winter
(C) extricate : entanglements
(D) digress : angst
(E) emulate : egotism

9 PASTICHE : WRITING ::

(A) collage : art
(B) melody : music
(C) bandage : medicine
(D) school : philosophy
(E) sequel : film

10 SIMIAN : APE ::

(A) feathered : vulture
(B) bovine : pasture
(C) infantile : child
(D) carnivorous : plant
(E) wizened : wisdom

11 LEVEE : FLOOD ::

(A) snow : avalanche
(B) rain : deluge
(C) immunization : disease
(D) zenith : view
(E) buttress : building

12 PURGATION : IMPURITIES ::

(A) catharsis : epiphanies
(B) sterilization : ailments
(C) salvation : prayers
(D) disinfection : bacteria
(E) inattention : details

13 PHILANTHROPIST : LARGESSE ::

(A) acrobat : net
(B) doctor : nurse
(C) mercenary : money
(D) professor : knowledge
(E) opportunist : advantage

1	A	B	C	D	E
2	A	B	C	D	E
3	A	B	C	D	E
4	A	B	C	D	E
5	A	B	C	D	E
6	A	B	C	D	E
7	A	B	C	D	E
8	A	B	C	D	E
9	A	B	C	D	E
10	A	B	C	D	E
11	A	B	C	D	E
12	A	B	C	D	E
13	A	B	C	D	E

WORDS YOU DIDN'T KNOW FROM PROBLEM SET 5

Before you check your answers below, take a minute to write down the words you didn't know from the previous questions. Look them up and review them tomorrow.

Word	Definition
____________	____________________
____________	____________________
____________	____________________
____________	____________________
____________	____________________
____________	____________________

Answers and Explanations: Problem Set 5

There are 13 analogies in this section, so we know that the first four will be relatively easy, the second five medium, and the last four relatively difficult. Did you remember not to skip any questions?

1 *C* A good sentence for this easy analogy is, "If you are *lame*, you have limited *mobility*," and the best answer is choice C: "If you are *hoarse*, you have limited *speech*."

2 *D* "*Bankruptcy* is a lack of *money*." The best answer is choice D: "*Apathy* is a lack of *caring*." Both choices A and E contain unrelated pairs.

3 *A* A good sentence here is, "An *asteroid* is a small *planet*," and the best answer was choice A: "A *quibble* is a small *objection*."

4 *E* "An *embargo* prevents *trade*," would be a good sentence, and the best answer is choice E: "A *helmet* prevents *injury*."

It sometimes happens that the sentence you come up with will work perfectly well with the capitalized words, and then appear not to work with any of the answer choices. For example, you might have made up the following sentence for this problem: "An *embargo* is a ban on *trade*." This is a fine sentence, but when you get to choice E it sounds less fine: "A *helmet* is a ban on *injury*." On the other hand, all the other choices sound even worse. At this point, you might try rewriting your sentence slightly to see if you can make the connection clearer.

5 *B* If your sentence is too vague (for example, "*alteration* is something you do to a *suit*,") then three of the answer choices (A, B, and C) appear to be possible. Therefore, we need a slightly more specific sentence: "An *alteration* is a change that someone makes to a *suit* to improve it." The best answer: "*Revision* is a change that someone makes to a *story* to improve it."

6 *B* A good sentence would be, "Someone who is *resolute* is full of *determination*." The best answer was choice B: "Someone who is *skeptical* is full of *doubt*." You might have been tempted momentarily by choice A, but in fact the words are basically unrelated. *Pristine* means "pure or unspoiled," while *grace* means "elegance."

7 *B* In case you were worried about picking three B's in a row, there can be as many as three of the same letter in a row, but never more than three.

A good sentence for the capitalized pair would be, "An *amplifier* helps you to hear something *inaudible*," and the best answer is choice B: "A *microscope* helps you to see something *imperceptible*." Choices A and C contain unrelated words, so we can eliminate them both.

8 *A* If you know the meaning of *vacillate* (and you should—it's one of the Hit Parade words and has already been used twice in this book), then a good sentence would be: "Someone who *vacillates* is filled with *indecision*."

If you don't know the meaning of *vacillate* yet, make a vow to learn it by tomorrow, and meanwhile, go straight to the answer choices. The first words in the answer choices are all verbs. Let's make some sentences:

(A) "To *lament* means to be full of *woe*." Could to *vacillate* mean to be full of *indecision*? Sure. Even if you weren't sure of the meaning of *vacillate*, this sentence might jar your memory. We'll hold on to this choice.

(B) "To *hibernate* means to sleep through the *winter*." Could to *vacillate* mean to sleep through *indecision*? No way.

(C) "To *extricate* means to get yourself out of *entanglements*." Could to *vacillate* mean to get yourself out of *indecision*? Possibly.

(D) *Digress* (meaning "to stray from the main idea") has nothing to do with *angst* (meaning "anxiety"), so this choice can be eliminated.

(E) *Emulate* (meaning "to copy") has nothing to do with *egotism*, so this too can be eliminated.

You're down to A and C. Can't decide which one to pick? You're *vacillating*!

9 *A* The more difficult the questions become, the more often you will have to go straight to the answer choices. If you knew the meaning of *pastiche*, your sentence would be, "A *pastiche* is a combination of several different kinds or styles of *writing*," and the correct answer would be choice A: "A *collage* is a combination of several different kinds of *art*."

If you didn't know the meaning of pastiche, you could first eliminate choice D, which contains an unrelated pair, and then work backward.

10 *C* Let's say you have no idea what *simian* means. Before we go to the answer choices, let's take stock of what we do know: *Simian* is an adjective that has something to do with the noun *ape*.

We can eliminate choices D and E because they contain unrelated pairs. Something that is *carnivorous* ("a meat-eater") can take or leave a *plant*. Something that is *wizened* ("old and shriveled") has nothing necessarily to do with *wisdom*.

Working backward from choice A, a good sentence would be "A *vulture*'s outer-body covering is *feathered*." Could an *ape*'s outer-body covering be *simian*?" Maybe. In choice B, *bovine* means "cow-like," which is only weakly related to *pasture*. In choice C, a good sentence would be, "*Infantile* behavior is *child*-like." Could *simian* behavior be *ape*-like? Well, yes. The definition of simian is "ape-like."

11 *C* Remember the floods in the Midwest in 1993? Along the riverbanks, volunteers constructed levees to hold back the water. A good sentence would be, "A *levee* holds back or prevents a *flood*."

In this case, *all* of the answer choices contain related pairs, so there is no elimination to be done that way. If you don't know the meaning of *levee*, you can work backward:

(A) "An *avalanche* is often composed of *snow*." Could a *flood* be composed of *levee*? This doesn't seem right.

(B) "A *deluge* is a lot of *rain*." Is a *flood* a lot of *levee*? Again, this doesn't sound correct. It is also hard to see how choice B could be the right answer without choice A being right as well, which basically eliminates both of them.

A further reason to eliminate both choices A and B is that the words *avalanche* and *deluge* both remind us a little too much of the word *flood*. We are looking for a relationship between pairs of words, not for individual words that seem similar. In this tough question, these are both probably Joe Bloggs answers!

(C) "*Immunization* prevents *disease*." Could a *levee* prevent a *flood*? We've already said that it could.

(D) "A *zenith* is a high place that might have a *view*." Does a *levee* have a *flood*? No, and besides, this relationship seems pretty weak.

(E) "A *buttress* is a supporting element of a *building*." Is a *levee* a supporting element of a *flood*? Nope.

The correct answer is choice C.

12 *D* While *purgation* may not be familiar to you, it might remind you of the word *purge*, especially since it is linked to *impurities*. To *purge* is to get rid of impurities, and thus a good sentence for the capitalized words would be, "*Purgation* is the process by which one gets rid of *impurities*." The best answer was choice D: "*Disinfection* is the process by which one gets rid of *bacteria*."

Catharsis is also a type of purging, but it is a purging of the emotions. *Epiphanies* are "sudden revelations." The two words are not necessarily related.

13 *D* This was your second opportunity to recognize the word *philanthropist*, a Hit Parade word. Did you remember the definition? You may not have run across *largesse* before, but before we go straight to the answer choices, let's review what we already know. The first word is *philanthropist*, someone who gives money or gifts to worthy causes. The second word is an unknown noun. It seems pretty likely that *largesse* is either another way of saying "money" or another way of saying "worthy causes."

Try saying it to yourself: "A *philanthropist* is someone who has a great deal of *largesse*." Or, backwards, "*Largesse* is a quality of a *Philantropist*."

Let's go to the answer choices.

(A) "An *acrobat* works over a *net* for safety." Does a *philanthropist* work over a *largesse* for safety? Not likely.

(B) "A *nurse* assists a *doctor*." Does a *largesse* assist a *philanthropist*? Probably not.

(C) "A *mercenary* is a soldier who fights for *money*." Does a *philanthropist* fight for *largesse*? Probably not.

(D) "A *professor* has a great of *knowledge*." Does a *philanthropist* have a great deal of *largesse*? Sounds possible.

(E) "An *opportunist* takes *advantage*." Does a *philanthropist* take *largesse*? Probably the other way around.

Largesse is the same thing as generosity and the correct answer is choice D.

4

Critical Reading

CRITICAL READING

All three of the verbal sections of the SAT contain critical reading passages. One of the 30-minute sections will contain one passage followed by up to 13 questions. The other 30-minute section will contain two passages with a total of up to 15 questions. There will be a third 15-minute section that will be entirely devoted to critical reading, with up to 13 more questions. One of the passages in one of these sections will be a "dual" passage, containing two separate passages giving contrasting viewpoints on one topic. Unlike the other questions on the SAT, critical reading questions are not arranged in order of difficulty. Instead, the questions are in rough chronological order. A question related to the first paragraph of a passage will come before a question about the second paragraph.

Let's begin by looking at a small section of a critical reading passage (and the questions that went with it) in a way that you won't see it on the real SAT—with the questions first:

Try answering the two questions below, based on the paragraph that follows.

5. The words "blotted out" in line 4 most nearly mean

(A) stained
(B) blemished
(C) obscured
(D) extinguished
(E) removed

6. The author mentions Sweden and Brazil in order to emphasize which point about the Krakatoa eruption?

(A) Although the eruption was devastating in Krakatoa, there were no effects felt in other parts of the word.
(B) The volcanic eruption was so powerful that it affected the climate of countries thousands of miles away.
(C) Local destruction in Krakatoa was enormous, but the destruction in Europe and South America was, if anything, greater.
(D) Brazil and Sweden had higher safety preparedness and thus escaped serious damage.
(E) The explosion would have been even more destructive had it happened today.

> The eruption of Krakatoa sent clouds of ash and dust into the Earth's atmosphere to a height of 50 miles. The sun was blotted out entirely for two days within a 100-mile radius of the volcano, and earth temperatures as far away as Sweden and Brazil were several degrees lower than average that year.

What do you notice? The answers to the above questions were located in specific places in the passages, and you didn't have to read the entire passage to get them right.

YOUR GOAL IS TO ANSWER QUESTIONS

No matter how much you pray, the proctor will not be walking around the examination room, saying, "Ah, Jessica! Excellent reading form. I'm giving you 20 extra points on your verbal score." The only way you get points in SAT critical reading is by correctly answering questions.

The sooner you get to the questions, the sooner you start earning points. For example, both of the questions on the previous page could be answered without reading the rest of the passage (which we didn't show you). In question 5, you needed to supply a word that would fit in place of the quoted words "blotted out." The best answer was choice C, "obscured," because the volcanic ash filled the sky to the point that the sun's rays couldn't get through. Even if you had read the entire passage several times and made extensive notes, the answer to this question was based on only one thing: your understanding of *this* sentence in *this* paragraph.

The best answer to question 6, which asked us why the author brought up Sweden and Brazil, was choice B. In the context of this paragraph, the two countries were mentioned to show just how powerful the eruption had been. Again, even if you had memorized the entire passage, the only place to find the answer to this question was right here in this paragraph.

These questions are pretty typical of the SAT in that they include either a line reference or an identification of the paragraph in which the answer can be found. Most of the questions in critical reading tell you where in the passage to look for the answer. You can find the answers to the other questions because the questions are arranged in chronological order. The answer to question number 3 will come between the answers to questions 2 and 4.

THEY'RE TOO LONG!

Many students look at a passage of 70 to 90 lines and feel defeated at the thought of trying to keep track of a passage this long—but the situation is much better than they think. Critical reading passages are actually a series of small paragraphs like the one you just read. Each of these paragraphs has a couple of very specific questions based on it. And when you answer these questions, all you have to think about is the paragraph in question.

THE PASSAGE TYPES

1. The Social Science Passage

This passage will be about a topic involving history, politics, economics, or sociology.

2. The Humanities Passage

This might range from an excerpt about an artist to an essay about literature, music, or philosophy.

3. The Science Passage

Usually not too dry, the science passage frequently involves a discussion of a scientific discovery, a new scientific theory, or a controversy in any of the scientific fields.

4. The Narrative Passage

Often an excerpt from a novel or short story, this type of passage frequently has actual dialogue, and is often the most fun to read.

5. The Dual Passage

One of the critical reading passages you will read during the SAT will actually be two shorter passages each taking a slightly different view on a related topic. The topics can be from any of the first three passage types.

While there are always four passages on the SAT (one of them a dual passage), there is no guarantee that you will definitely see one of each of the types just mentioned. For example, several recent tests have contained no narrative passage at all, with an extra humanities or sociology passage to make up for it.

One of the four passages will probably concern a minority or ethnic group.

THE PRINCETON REVIEW METHOD

Remember that the only way to get points in critical reading is by correctly answering questions. This is why you should have only three goals when you read the passage:

1. Read the "blurb" (the introductory sentence which describes the passage).
2. Go to the questions and figure out what parts of the passage you need to read.
3. Read just what you need to find the answer and get your points.

Almost every question will give you a line number or a lead word that will tell you where to look in the passage for your answer. Read just those parts, and if ETS *does* ask the question, they will include a line number so that you can go back and read about it as carefully as you like.

THE QUESTION TYPES

1. Line Reference and Lead Word Questions

The majority of the Critical Reading questions will be line reference or lead word questions. In each case, the question will tell you where in the passage to look for the answer.

Line reference questions ask you about a part of the passage and tell you which lines the question refers to. These questions will look like one of the following:

> In paragraph 4, why does the author mention Harry McCallan?
>
> The author cites "many interesting creatures" on lines 34-36 in order to . . .

Sometimes, instead of a line or paragraph number, you will be asked about a proper name or important word that will be pretty easy to find in the passage by running your finger down the passage until you come across it. We call these "lead words."

In either case, you should look back to the passage and find the lines indicated by the question or the lines in which the lead word can be found. It's important to read a little above and a little below the line number mentioned or the line on which the lead word, to make sure you understand the line in context. Then you need to pick the answer that best re-states what the passage itself says on those lines.

From time to time, you will see a question that seems specific, even though it has neither a line reference nor a colorful word to help you find the reference in the passage. It's not a bad idea to skip a question like this until after you've answered the rest of the questions and have a better understanding of the passage. Remember, however, that the questions are arranged chronologically. If this is question 3, then the information you need to answer it will probably be found right after the information needed to answer question 2 and right before the information needed to answer question 4.

2. Vocabulary-In-Context Questions

Vocabulary in-context questions always include a line number and ask you to pick an alternate word for the quoted word or phrase. Here's what they look like:

> In line 44, "objective" most nearly means. . .

The thing to bear in mind in these questions is that ETS often picks words that have more than one meaning, and the words are generally not being used in their primary sense. For example, ETS's answer to the question above about the meaning of the word "objective" was the word "material"— certainly not the first meaning anyone would think of picking.

The best way to approach these questions is to cover up the answer choices and try to fill in your *own* word first.

If you find yourself running out of time as you get to a critical reading passage (and as we said in the introduction, it makes sense for most people to leave critical reading for last after analogies and sentence completions) then these are the questions to answer first. Not only do they take the least amount of time but they also require the smallest amount of overall knowledge of the passage.

3. General Questions

Usually there will be one general question per passage. It will probably look like one of the following:

> The main idea of this passage is to
>
> The primary purpose of the passage is to
>
> The passage is best described as
>
> The passage serves primarily to
>
> The author uses the example of the [Krakatoa eruption] primarily to

We suggest that you save the General questions for last. By the time you have answered all of the Line Reference and Lead Word questions, you will have read enough of the passage that you will probably have a good idea of the main point. If not, try going back and re-reading the opening line of each paragraph. It's a good bet that these lines will be a good paraphrase of the main idea.

DUAL PASSAGES

One of the passages on your SAT will actually be two shorter passages giving two perspectives on one topic, followed by up to 13 questions. Recent dual passages have given two views of architecture in cities, two views on the jazz saxophonist Miles Davis, and two views on whether controversial books should be banned. Although the double passage is generally located in the15-minute section of the SAT, it doesn't have to be. Wherever it is, you should tackle it in the following way:

1) Answer the questions based on the first passage.
2) Answer the questions based on the second passage.
3) Finally, answer the questions that refer to both passages.

PACING STRATEGIES FOR CRITICAL READING

In the 30-question verbal section, there are always two passages. Most students just start with the first one, but it's worth taking a few seconds to scope out both passages and begin with the one whose tone you like best. If you are shooting for a score of 200 to 390, all you need to answer is one passage worth of questions—you can skip the other passage entirely. If you are shooting for a score of 400 to 490, you need to answer about half of the questions in the second passage as well. In this case, which questions should you go for in the second passage? Vocabulary and specific line number questions are usually the easiest. If you get into time trouble, you can actually go straight to the questions and not bother skimming the passage at all. If you are shooting for a score of 500 and above, you will need to answer virtually all the questions, but it still pays to begin with the passage you think you'll enjoy better.

In the 35-question section, there is only one passage (although it might be a "dual passage"). If you are shooting for a score between 200 and 290, you don't have to do any critical reading at all. If you're shooting for a score between 300 and 390, you only need to answer half the questions based on this passage. If you are shooting for a score above 400, you should try to answer all of these questions.

In the 15-minute, 13-question section, there is only one passage (although, again, it might be a "dual passage"). If you are shooting for a score of 200 to 290 you need to answer about six of the questions. If you're shooting for a 300 to a 490, you should answer about 10 questions. If you're shooting for anything above a 500, you need to answer all the questions.

CRITICAL READING CHECKLIST

1. Read the beginning blurb.

2. Answer the Line Reference and Lead Word questions. Remember to read above and below the specified lines to understand their context. For other specific questions that don't have a line reference, use chronology to figure out where the answer will be found in the passage.

3. Answer the Vocabulary-in-Context questions.

4. Answer any General questions.

5. With dual passages, read the first passage first, and answer all questions relating to that passage. Then read the second passage and answer all questions related to that passage. Finally, do the questions related to both passages. These are always at the end.

CRITICAL READING: PRACTICE PASSAGE 1

Using the information contained in the passage and the introductory material below, answer the questions that follow.

Recommended time: This drill is untimed.

Questions 1-7 are based on the following passage.

The following passage gives a critical overview of the work of Frank Lloyd Wright, one of America's most famous architects.

It is 30 years since Frank Lloyd Wright died at ninety-one and it is no exaggeration to say that the United States has had no architect even roughly comparable to him since. His extraordinary 72-year career spanned the shingled Hillside Home school in Wisconsin in 1887 to the Guggenheim Museum built in New York in 1959.

His great early work, the prairie houses of the Midwest in which he developed his style of open, flowing space and great horizontal panes and integrated structure of wood, stone, glass, and stucco were mostly built before 1910, and Philip Johnson once insulted Wright by calling him "America's greatest nineteenth-century architect." But Mr. Johnson was then a partisan of the sleek, austere International Style which Wright abhorred. Now, the International Style is in disarray, and what is significant here is that Wright's reputation has not suffered much at all in the current antimodernist upheaval.

One of the reasons that Wright's reputation has not suffered too severely in the current turmoil in architectural thinking is that he spoke a tremendous amount of common sense. He was full of ideas which seemed daring, almost absurd, but which now in retrospect were clearly right. Back in the 1920's, for example, he alone among architects and planners perceived the great effect the automobile would have on the American landscape. He foresaw "the great highway becoming, and rapidly, the horizontal line of a new freedom extending from ocean to ocean," as he wrote in his autobiography of 1932. Wright wrote approvingly of the trend toward decentralization, which hardly endears him to today's center-city-minded planners—but if his calls toward suburban planning had been realized, the chaotic sprawl of the American landscape might today have some rational order to it.

Wright was obsessed with the problem of the affordable house for the middle-class American. It may be that no other prominent architect has ever designed as many prototypes of inexpensive houses that could be mass-produced; unlike most current high stylists, who ignore the boredom of suburban tract houses and design expensive custom residences in the hope of establishing a distance between themselves and mass culture, Wright tried hard to close the gap between the architectural profession and the general public.

In his modest houses or his grand ones, Wright emphasized appropriate materials, which might well be considered to prefigure both the growing preoccupation today with energy-saving design and the surge of interest in regional architecture. Wright, unlike the architects of the International Style, would not build the same house in Massachusetts that he would build in California; he was concerned about local traditions, regional climates, and so forth. It is perhaps no accident that at Wright's Scottsdale, Arizona home and studio that continues to function, many of the younger architects have begun doing solar designs as a logical step from Wright's work.

1 The phrase "comparable to" (line 5) most nearly means

(A) as good as
(B) similar to
(C) like
(D) related to
(E) associated with

2 According to the passage, Wright's typical style included all of the following EXCEPT:

(A) the integrated use of different types of building materials
(B) open flowing spaces
(C) large horizontal panes
(D) solar-powered heating systems
(E) regional architectural elements

3 Philip Johnson's quotation about Wright (lines 17-18) was an insult because

(A) Wright did not respect Johnson's opinion
(B) Johnson was a rival architect who wanted the title for himself
(C) it ignored the many famous buildings that Wright built in the twentieth century
(D) Johnson's International Style has since fallen out of favor
(E) Wright was an elderly man and deserved to be treated with more respect

4 In the third paragraph, the author mentions Wright's thoughts about the importance of the automobile primarily to illustrate

(A) the general mood of the times
(B) Wright's ability to correctly predict the future
(C) the absurdity of Wright's ideas
(D) the need for centralization in America
(E) Wright's somewhat egotistical demeanor

5 According to the passage, Wright foresaw that "the great effect" of the automobile (lines 35-36) would be to

(A) increase the number of highways in America
(B) enhance the need for solar-powered designs
(C) create decentralized suburban communities
(D) reduce the number of city planners
(E) weaken the International Style, an architectural movement of which Wright disapproved.

6 In lines 57-58, the phrase "who ignore the boredom of suburban tract houses" most closely means the architects

(A) find these houses to be in bad taste
(B) are sympathetic to the plight of the poor
(C) are willing to overlook the financial limitations of designing houses that could be mass-produced
(D) design expensive, stylized homes for the masses
(E) do not want to be bothered with designing inexpensive homes

7 Wright's refusal to build an identical house in both Massachusetts and California (lines 73-75) came out of his conviction that

(A) each house should be a unique design, never to be duplicated
(B) only International Style homes could be duplicated anywhere
(C) each design should reflect features of regional architecture and climate concerns
(D) he would only design for midwestern locations
(E) although he designed homes for mass-production, he felt others should do the actual duplication

1 ⊂A⊃ ⊂B⊃ ⊂C⊃ ⊂D⊃ ⊂E⊃
2 ⊂A⊃ ⊂B⊃ ⊂C⊃ ⊂D⊃ ⊂E⊃
3 ⊂A⊃ ⊂B⊃ ⊂C⊃ ⊂D⊃ ⊂E⊃
4 ⊂A⊃ ⊂B⊃ ⊂C⊃ ⊂D⊃ ⊂E⊃
5 ⊂A⊃ ⊂B⊃ ⊂C⊃ ⊂D⊃ ⊂E⊃
6 ⊂A⊃ ⊂B⊃ ⊂C⊃ ⊂D⊃ ⊂E⊃
7 ⊂A⊃ ⊂B⊃ ⊂C⊃ ⊂D⊃ ⊂E⊃

Answers and Explanations: Practice Passage 1

As you read the passage, you are looking for the main idea of the passage and a general sense of what is going on in the individual paragraphs. The italicized introductory material told us this would be an overview of the work of a famous architect, but it was not until we read the first paragraph that we knew how the author felt about Wright: The first paragraph could be summarized as, "Wright is great!" The second paragraph is devoted to his early work. The third paragraph is about his common sense and his foresight. The fourth paragraph concerns his attempts to design affordable homes for the middle class. The fifth paragraph speaks of how his designs prefigured today's concerns with regional architecture and energy-saving design.

Now, let's attack the questions.

1 *A* From the blurb, you know that this passage is basically about the famous architect. Reading the entire sentence in which the quoted word appears, it's clear the author is saying that no other architect has come close to being as good as Wright. Thus, it is not enough to use the words in choices B or C. We need something stronger. Choices D and E, which merely say there have been no architects connected to Wright, seem both factually incorrect (based on what we learn later in the passage) and inconsistent with the intended meaning of the sentence. The best answer is choice A.

2 *D* You may have initially skipped this question because it did not contain a line reference, while many of the other questions did. However, this being the second question, we can assume that the answer will be found somewhere near the beginning of the passage. In this case, the answers (correct and incorrect) could be found in lines 10-14 at the beginning of the second paragraph.

Remember, this is an EXCEPT question, so we are looking for the one answer that is NOT true. Choices A, B, and C were easy to find in the lines we just mentioned. Choices D and E seem less obvious. Did Wright's homes use solar power? Much later in the passage, the author says that his later disciples used solar power in their designs as a kind of logical extension of Wright's principles, but nowhere is it stated that Wright himself used solar heating. Wright's taste for regional elements is spoken of later as well, but we get a good hint of this in the lines already cited, where the author speaks of Wright's "prairie houses of the Midwest." The best answer is choice D.

3 *C* This question was a little tough because the answer was not completely spelled out. In the previous paragraph we had been told that Wright designed buildings from the 1880s through at least 1959 when he designed the famous Guggenheim Museum. Obviously, most of his designs were done during the 20th century. Thus, Johnson was putting Wright down by implying that his only important work had taken place very early in his career.

Because this was a subtle point, you may have been better off eliminating incorrect answer choices.

(A) If Wright really didn't respect Johnson's opinion, then he wouldn't have been very insulted by Johnson's comment.

(B) The fact that Johnson was a jealous rival would not explain why his seeming compliment was in fact an insult.

(D) Why would what later happened to Johnson's movement have anything to do with his statement being an insult?

(E) This is a possible answer, but we actually have no way of knowing when Johnson made the statement—Wright might still have been a relatively young man when it was made.

TIP: Read a few lines above and below the quoted lines to understand the context.

4 *B* As always, you should read the paragraph not only for the sentences related to the automobile, but for the context in which those sentences are presented. A bit earlier in the paragraph, the author says, "He was full of ideas which seemed daring, almost absurd, but (**trigger word**) which now in retrospect were clearly right." The automobile sentences are presented as an example of Wright's foresight. The correct answer is choice B. Choice A is a little too vague. If you chose choice C, you missed the trigger word. Choice D gets the meaning wrong: Wright favored decentralization. If you chose E, you might well have been correct about his demeanor, but you didn't get it from this passage. Be careful about outside information.

5 *C* It's always great when two questions refer to the same patch of passage—you've just been reading and thinking about these sentences in order to answer question 4. The beginning of the sentence that contained the quote stated, ". . . he alone among architects and planners perceived...." Thus, he was thinking about these issues as an architect. What relevance could the expansion away from cities have on an architect? This expansion would lead to an expansion of suburban communities. This is spelled out further toward the end of the paragraph. Choice A would have little effect on an architect. Choice B speaks of a design that was not possible during Wright's lifetime. Choices D and E might both be true, but neither was stated in the passage. The correct answer is choice C.

6 *E* In this paragraph, Wright is set in opposition to most current architects. Note the trigger word in the following sentence: "Unlike (**trigger word**) most current high stylists, who ignore the boredom of suburban tract houses..., Wright tried hard to close the gap between the architectural profession and the general public." Wright was designing for the common person; most current architects are not. Thus choices B, C, and D can be eliminated—D because the masses can't afford expensive homes. Choice A got these architects' distaste right, but didn't catch the intention of the passage to portray them as not wishing to get involved in the business of mass-produced homes. The best answer is choice E.

7 *C* The answer to this question came from the sentences immediately before and immediately after the quoted lines. "Local traditions and regional climates" were Wright's reasons for not duplicating houses in different parts of the country.

CRITICAL READING: PRACTICE PASSAGE 2

Using the information contained in the passage and introductory material below, answer the questions that follow.

Recommended time: about 7 minutes

Questions 1-7 are based on the following passage.

Many articles and books have been written proposing a major revamping of the nation's school system. In this excerpt, the author presents his own views on this subject.

When nearly everybody agrees on something it probably isn't so. Nearly everybody agrees; it's going to take a revolution to fix America's public schools. From the great national think tanks to the neighborhood PTA, the call to the barricades is being trumpeted. Louis V. Gerstner Jr., head of RJR Nabisco and one of the business leaders in education reform, proclaims the Noah Principle: "No more prizes for predicting rain. Prizes only for building arks. We've got to change whole schools, and the whole school system."

But it isn't so; most of that is just rhetoric. In the first place, nobody really wants a revolution. Revolution would mean junking the whole present structure of education overnight and inventing a new one from scratch, in the giddy conviction that anything must be an improvement—no matter what it costs in terms of untaught kids, wrecked careers and doomed experiments. What these folks really want isn't revolution but major reform, changing the system radically but in an orderly fashion. The changes are supposed to be tested in large-scale pilot programs—Gertner's "arks"—and then installed nationally.

But even that is just a distant gleam in the eye, and a dubious proposition too. There's nothing like a consensus even on designing those arks, let alone where they are supposed to come to ground. And anyone who has watched radical reforms in the real world has to be wary of them: Invariably, they take a long time and cost a great deal, and even so they fail more often than they succeed. In organizations as in organisms, evolution works best a step at a time. The best and most natural changes come not in wholesale gulps, but in small bites.

What the big-think reformers fail to acknowledge is that schools all over the country are changing all the time. From head-start programs to after-school big brother/big sister projects to self-esteem workshops, it's precisely these small-scale innovations and demonstration programs that are doing the job, in literally thousands of schools. Some of these efforts are only partly successful; some fail; some work small miracles. They focus varyingly on children, teachers and parents, on methods of administration and techniques of teaching, on efforts to motivate kids and to teach values and to mobilize community support. Some are relatively expensive, others cost almost nothing. But all of them can be done— and have been done.

The important thing is that local schools aren't waiting for a revolution, or for gurus to decree the new model classroom from sea to shining sea. They are working out their own problems and making their own schools better. And anyone—teachers, parents, principals, school board members—anyone who cares enough and works hard enough can do the same.

1 The primary purpose of the passage is to

(A) present an alternative view on a widely-held belief
(B) refute the notion that change of any kind is needed
(C) describe several plans to implement an educational revolution
(D) uncover and analyze new flaws in an old system
(E) relate the historical events that have shaped a situation

2 The quotation in lines 11-14 ("No more prizes...arks.") can best be interpreted to mean that Gerstner believes

(A) the present school system is functioning adequately
(B) rather than focus on describing problems, the emphasis should be shifted to finding solutions
(C) the author of the passage is a religious person
(D) school curriculum should include more classes on topics such as shipbuilding, and fewer classes on meteorology
(E) in the value of monetary prizes to outstanding students

3 The author views the pilot programs mentioned in lines 28-45 as which of the following?

I. Costly and time-consuming
II. A product of consensus
III. Uncertain to succeed

(A) I only
(B) II only
(C) III only
(D) I and III only
(E) I, II, and III

4 In line 44, "wholesale" most nearly means

(A) cheap
(B) fair
(C) large
(D) valuable
(E) intensive

5 Which best summarizes the idea of "small bites" (line 44-45)?

(A) Changing the system radically but in an orderly fashion.
(B) Making the system gradually look more like it did in the past.
(C) Allowing children to choose from a variety of programs.
(D) Teaching the theory of evolution in the classroom.
(E) Using modest innovations to improve schools.

6 According to the author, the "small-scale innovations" referred to in lines 51-52

(A) are largely theoretical so far
(B) are producing a revolution in education
(C) have in many cases been shown to work
(D) do not work on a large scale
(E) are unavailable in many areas

7 Judging from the author's discussion, he believes that local schools

(A) should embrace sweeping plans for national educational reform
(B) are relatively expensive
(C) can only be as good as their curricula
(D) are producing small but useful innovations all the time
(E) will fall victim to doomed experiments

1 ⊂A⊃ ⊂B⊃ ⊂C⊃ ⊂D⊃ ⊂E⊃
2 ⊂A⊃ ⊂B⊃ ⊂C⊃ ⊂D⊃ ⊂E⊃
3 ⊂A⊃ ⊂B⊃ ⊂C⊃ ⊂D⊃ ⊂E⊃
4 ⊂A⊃ ⊂B⊃ ⊂C⊃ ⊂D⊃ ⊂E⊃
5 ⊂A⊃ ⊂B⊃ ⊂C⊃ ⊂D⊃ ⊂E⊃
6 ⊂A⊃ ⊂B⊃ ⊂C⊃ ⊂D⊃ ⊂E⊃
7 ⊂A⊃ ⊂B⊃ ⊂C⊃ ⊂D⊃ ⊂E⊃

Answers and Explanations: Practice Passage 2

1 *A* This general question asks you for the main idea of the passage—which you probably figured out while answering the other questions. In this case, the blurb tells you everything you need to know: We are told that the author is presenting an alternate view. To confirm this, look at the first paragraph; it tells us what "everybody agrees about." Then, in the second paragraph, after the trigger word "but," we find out what the author thinks instead. Choice B is contrary to the passage itself. No large-scale programs are described in the passage, so choice C can be eliminated. Choices D and E are also somewhat contrary to the intent of the passage. The best answer is choice A.

2 *B* As always, when ETS gives you specific lines to look at, you should remember to read above and below the quote to get a sense of the purpose of the entire paragraph. The paragraph as a whole is describing what "everybody" thinks they want: a revolution in the way children are taught. Gerstner is quoted as representing this feeling. Thus choice A can be eliminated immediately; Gerstner wants radical change. It is unclear whether Gerstner is even aware of the author's existence, thus choice C is impossible. Choices D and E take the quotation too literally. Gerstner is making a metaphorical point. The best answer is choice B.

3 *D* While the pilot programs are mentioned at the end of paragraph 2, the answer to this question comes at the beginning of paragraph 3. In line 38, the author says, ". . .they take a long time and cost a great deal, and even so they fail more often than they succeed." A bit earlier in the paragraph, it says, "there's nothing like a consensus even on designing those arks, let alone . . ."

Let's look at the choices. Roman numeral I was definitely said, so we can eliminate any answer choice that does not include I. Choices B and C bite the dust. Roman numeral II gets the author's thoughts backward, so we can eliminate any choice that includes II; choice E can be crossed off. Roman numeral III was also definitely stated, so the best answer is choice D.

4 *C* Specific line vocabulary questions are normally quick to do, but as always, beware of secondary and far-fetched definitions. In other contexts, "wholesale" might mean cheap or fair, but in this case, the best answer is choice C. We can get this from the context of the rest of the sentence: "Not in _______ gulps, but in <u>small</u> bites."

5 *E* The answer to this question can be found in paragraph 4, line 51: ". . . it's precisely these small-scale innovations. . .that are doing the job. . . ." You might not have realized where you needed to look to find this answer, but you could have eliminated several of the answer choices anyway. Since the author does not favor revolution, we can eliminate choice A. Since the author is proposing small changes, we can eliminate choice B. Choice C is not mentioned in the passage at all. Choice D is a trap answer for anyone who noticed the word evolution right in front of the quoted lines. However, the author is speaking of the evolution of the school system, not evolution as it is taught (or not taught) in the schools. The best answer is choice E.

6 *C* You may have noticed that questions 5, 6, and 7 all referred to the same paragraph, which is great! By now, you must be an expert on paragraph 4. Reading from the beginning of the paragraph in which the quoted words appear, we see that "schools. . . are changing all the time." Then a bit later, we see that "it's precisely these small-scale innovations. . .that are doing the job in . . . thousands of schools. . . ." Thus, the innovations are not theoretical (cross off choice A), or revolutionary (cross off choice B), or unavailable in many areas (cross off choice E). We don't have any information on whether they will work on a large scale, so the best answer is choice C.

7 *D* Since this question did not have a specific line number, you may have initially skipped it. However, if you had looked toward the end of the passage for the lead words, "local schools," the answer was to be found at the beginning of the fourth paragraph. "Schools all over the country are changing all the time." Choice A is clearly against the author's stated preference. Choices B and C are not mentioned in the passage. Choice E is a trap answer based on language in paragraph 2. The best answer is choice D.

CRITICAL READING: PRACTICE PASSAGE 3

Using the information contained in the passage and introductory material below, answer the questions that follow.

Recommended time: about 8 minutes

Questions 1-7 are based on the following passage.

Scientists, theologians, and lay persons have debated the origins of life on Earth for hundreds of years. The following passage presents one scientist's explanation.

How did the earliest, most primitive, forms of life begin? Let's start with the formation of the earth 4.5 billion years ago. We can allow the first few hundred million years to pass while the Earth settles down to more or less its present state. It cools down and squeezes out an ocean and an atmosphere. The surrounding hydrogen is swept away by the solar wind, and the rain of meteors out of which the Earth was formed dwindles and virtually ceases.

Then, perhaps 4,000 million years ago, the Earth is reasonably quiet and the period of "chemical evolution" begins. The first live molecules are small ones made up of two to five atoms each—the simplest form of life we can imagine—a single-strand RNA molecule.

Different scientific theories have been proposed as to how this molecule first came into being. In 1908 the Swedish chemist Svante August Arrhenius theorized that life on Earth began when spores (living, but capable of very long periods of suspended animation) drifted across space for millions of years, perhaps until some landed on our planet and were brought back to active life by its gentle environment.

This is highly dramatic, but even if we imagine that Earth was seeded from another world, which, long, long before, had been seeded from still another world, we must still come back to some period when life began on some world through spontaneous generation—and we may as well assume that this generation began on Earth.

Why not? Even if spontaneous generation does not (or, possibly, cannot) take place on Earth now, conditions on the primordial Earth were so different that what seems a firm rule now may not have been so firm then.

What won't happen spontaneously may well happen if energy is supplied. In the primordial Earth, there were energy sources—volcanic heat, lightning, and most of all, sunshine. At that time, the Earth's atmosphere did not contain oxygen, or its derivative, ozone, and the Sun's energetic ultraviolet rays would reach the Earth's surface undiluted.

In 1954 a chemistry student, Stanley Lloyd Miller, made a fascinating discovery that shed light on the passage from a substance that is definitely unliving to one that is, in however simple a fashion, alive. He began with a mixture of water, ammonia, methane, and hydrogen (materials he believed to have been present on the Earth at its beginning). He made sure his mixture was sterile and had no life of any kind in it. He then circulated it past an electric discharge (to mimic the energy sources roiling the planet at that time.) At the end of a week, he analyzed his solution and found that some of its small molecules had been built up to larger ones. Among these larger molecules were glycine and alanine, the two simplest of the twenty amino acids. This was the first proof that organic material could have been formed from the inanimate substances that existed on Earth so long ago.

1 In the first paragraph, the author discusses the "first few hundred million years" after the Earth was formed in order to

(A) illustrate two theories as to how the Earth was created

(B) demonstrate how hardy living organisms had to be to survive this initial period
(C) describe the Earth as it was before life began
(D) discredit the theory that life had an extra-terrestrial origin
(E) explain the concept of spontaneous generation

2 The author most likely views the theories of Svante August Arrhenius as

(A) innovative and daring
(B) dramatic but logical
(C) interesting but unlikely
(D) impossible and illogical
(E) lunatic and unscientific

3 The word "generation" in line 37 most nearly means

(A) descendants
(B) development
(C) offspring
(D) designation
(E) period

4 According to the passage, the "energy" mentioned in lines 46-54 may have been important for which of the following reasons?

(A) Sources of energy found at that time produced the oxygen in Earth's atmosphere.
(B) This energy may have helped to promote spontaneous generation.
(C) It was more powerful than volcanic heat and ultra-violet rays at that time.
(D) Ultra-violet energy converted oxygen into ozone.
(E) It mimicked exactly the energy of electric discharge.

5 In line 54, the word "undiluted" most nearly means

(A) purified
(B) condensed
(C) watered down
(D) unweakened
(E) untested

6 The author uses the example of Stanley Miller's experiment primarily to suggest

(A) a laboratory confirmation of the theoretical possibility of spontaneous generation
(B) the need for further research in this field
(C) a discovery of the list of materials that were present when the Earth was first created
(D) that amino acids are not, in fact, building blocks of organic materials
(E) the possibility of an extra-terrestrial source for the first organic matter on Earth

7 The author's conclusion at the end of the last paragraph would be most directly supported by additional information concerning

(A) what other chemical materials were present on the Earth 4 billion years ago
(B) why life did not begin during the first few hundred million years after the Earth formed
(C) whether other chemistry professors were able to recreate the same results attained by Miller
(D) how Arrhenius went about his search for spores in meteorites
(E) why hydrogen in the Earth's atmosphere was removed by solar wind

1 ⊂A⊃ ⊂B⊃ ⊂C⊃ ⊂D⊃ ⊂E⊃
2 ⊂A⊃ ⊂B⊃ ⊂C⊃ ⊂D⊃ ⊂E⊃
3 ⊂A⊃ ⊂B⊃ ⊂C⊃ ⊂D⊃ ⊂E⊃
4 ⊂A⊃ ⊂B⊃ ⊂C⊃ ⊂D⊃ ⊂E⊃
5 ⊂A⊃ ⊂B⊃ ⊂C⊃ ⊂D⊃ ⊂E⊃
6 ⊂A⊃ ⊂B⊃ ⊂C⊃ ⊂D⊃ ⊂E⊃
7 ⊂A⊃ ⊂B⊃ ⊂C⊃ ⊂D⊃ ⊂E⊃

Answers and Explanations: Practice Passage 3

1 *C* We know from the introductory blurb that the passage will be about a theory that explains the origin of life on Earth, not the origin of the Earth itself. Certainly there were not two theories presented. Thus we can eliminate choice A. Choice B, while seemingly plausible, is wrong because even the beginnings of primitive life on Earth do not start until later, according to the second paragraph. Choice C correctly describes the purpose of this description: to set the scene for the "chemical evolution" that was about to begin. Extra-terrestrial origins were not brought up until the third paragraph, so we can eliminate choice D. If you chose choice E, you were thinking too much. Ultimately, the entire passage is helping to explain spontaneous generation, but the specific purpose of paragraph 1 is best described by choice C.

2 *C* Where do we find Arrhenius? Paragraph 3—but the author's reaction to Arrhenius is in paragraph 4. The trigger word ("but") in the middle of the first sentence tells us that the author does not totally buy Arrhenius's theory, which gets rid of choices A and B. On the other hand, does the author think he's a crackpot? No, which allows us to get rid of choices D and E. The best answer is choice C.

3 *B* Specific line vocabulary questions are easy in that you know right where to look, and you don't have to read much beyond the sentence before and after the quoted word. But they're tough in that the definitions are not always exactly what you'd expect, and often entail secondary meanings. For example, here the word "generation" can mean descendants or offspring or even possibly period—but none of these is right in this case. The "generation" that's being talked about is "spontaneous generation" as it is being discussed in this passage: the starting spark of primitive life where none existed before. Choice B is the best answer.

4 *B* The entire passage is about the origin of primitive life on Earth. The paragraph in question is describing how this spontaneous generation might happen—by the application of various kinds of energy. If you didn't notice this while you were doing the question, you still could have eliminated a few of the other answer choices:

(A) It was the lack of oxygen at that time that helped to let one form of energy (ultraviolet rays from sunlight) through to the surface of the planet. Eliminate.

(C) The energy referred to in the question included volcanic heat and ultra-violet rays. Cross it off.

(D) The paragraph didn't say this. Cross it off.

(E) Just the opposite—the electric discharge described in the next paragraph was used by Miller to mimic the primordial energy. Eliminate.

The best answer was choice B.

5 *D* Oxygen and ozone in the Earth's atmosphere dilute the sun's rays so that they are less powerful. Four billion years ago, there was no oxygen or ozone, and so these rays were not weakened. The best answer is choice D.

6 *A* There is no line number here, but by scanning for the lead words "Stanley Miller" we will find the answer in the last paragraph. The topic sentence of the paragraph gives it all away: ". . . Miller made a fascinating discovery that shed light on the passage from a substance that is definitely unliving to one that is, in however simple a fashion, alive." His experiment helped to confirm the explanation of the origins of primitive life (spontaneous generation) that the author describes in this passage. The best answer is choice A. We could eliminate choice B because, while there is always a need for further research, this need was not mentioned at all in the passage. Miller's choice of materials may have been based on a new discovery, but again this was not the central point of the passage, so we can cross off choice C. Choice D contradicts the author. Miller's experiment tends to contradict choice E: Miller tried to recreate the chemicals and the energy that existed on Earth at that time.

7 *C* Miller's results wouldn't be worth much unless they could be corroborated, and this was why choice C was best. Choices B, D, and E addressed issues that were brought up in earlier paragraphs, and had little bearing on spontaneous generation. It might be interesting to know what other chemicals were present, but as long as these chemicals were present, then the experiment is valid. The best answer is choice C.

CRITICAL READING: PRACTICE PASSAGE 4

Using the information contained in the passage and introductory material below, answer the questions that follow.

Recommended time: about 7 minutes

Questions 1-6 are based on the following passage.

The following passage is an excerpt from a memoir written by writer John Burke, about the novelist Joseph Heller.

I became a fan of Joseph Heller's writing while I was a student in high school in the 1970s. His most famous book, *Catch-22*, was practically an anthem for myself and my friends. We had dissected it, sitting in the park outside school, reciting certain key passages aloud and proclaiming to anyone who would listen that this was quite possibly the best book ever written. Nearly twenty years later I am not sure that we were wrong.

Heller created a modern-day anti-hero who was a soldier trying to stay sane in the midst of a war in which he no longer believed. This spoke to my generation, growing up as we did during the turmoil of Vietnam, and—however you felt about the issue—his ideas were considered important.

I had spent many hours imagining what the man who had created the savage wit and brilliant imagery of that book would be like in person. I was soon to find out. To this day, I have no idea how it was arranged, but somehow an invitation to speak at my high school was extended, and duly accepted.

On the day, I made sure to be near the gate of the school to see him arrive. I was looking for a limousine, or perhaps an entourage of reporters surrounding the man whose dust-jacket picture I had scrutinized so often. But suddenly, there he was, completely alone, walking hesitantly toward the school like just a normal person. He walked by me, and I was amazed to see that he was wearing rather tattered sneakers, down at the heel.

When he began speaking in the auditorium, I was dumbfounded, for he had a very heavy speech impediment.

"That can't be him," I whispered loudly to a friend. "He sounds like a dork."

My notions of a brilliant man at that time did not extend to a speech impediment—or any handicap whatsoever. Ordinary people were handicapped, but not men of brilliance. There was, in fact, a fair amount of whispering going on in the auditorium.

And then somehow, we began to listen to what he was saying. He was completely brilliant. He seemed to know just what we were thinking and articulated feelings that I had only barely known that I had. He spoke for 40 minutes and held us all spell-bound. I would not have left my seat even if I could.

As I listened, I began to feel awaken in me the possibility of being more than I had supposed that I could be. With some difficulty I managed to get to the school gate again, and waited for twenty minutes while I suppose he signed autographs and fielded questions inside the auditorium. Eventually, he came out, as he had come in, alone.

I screwed up all my courage and called to him, "Mr. Heller."

He almost didn't stop but then he turned around and came over to me.

"I just wanted to say how much I enjoyed your book. "

He looked down at me in my wheelchair, smiled as if it was the most normal thing in the world, and shook my hand. I think that day may have been very important in the future direction of my life.

1 To the author, Joseph Heller's novel, *Catch-22* was

(A) an important but little-known work
(B) unusual in its frank portrayal of high school students and their problems
(C) too traditional for most readers
(D) inspiring and thought-provoking
(E) more suited to an older generation

2 The primary purpose of the passage is to

(A) describe an event that may have changed the author's perception of himself
(B) profile a famous novelist
(C) relate in dramatic form the author's early childhood memories
(D) suggest the sense of disappointment the author felt at encountering his hero in person
(E) discuss the literary significance of Heller's most famous novel

3 The description of Heller's sneakers in lines 39-40 provides all of the following EXCEPT

(A) a contrast between the actual appearance of Heller and the author's image of him
(B) a telling detail about Joseph Heller
(C) a revealing insight into the mind of the author at that time
(D) a suggestion that Heller may have been dressing down deliberately to put his young audience at ease
(E) information to suggest that Heller had owned the sneakers for some time

4 The author describes Heller's speech (lines 41-62), primarily in order to

(A) illustrate the wit and imagery of the novelist's ideas
(B) describe the disappointment of the high school kids at the inarticulateness of the speaker
(C) respond to charges that Heller's work is overrated
(D) show that the students' initial skepticism was overcome by their interest in what he was saying
(E) demonstrate the lack of respect that was shown to the novelist because of his speech impediment

5 The word "fielded," in line 69, most nearly means

(A) evaded
(B) asked
(C) responded to
(D) delved into
(E) caught

6 The author most likely remembers his handshake with Heller because

(A) Heller almost didn't stop to shake his hand
(B) it was a form of recognition from someone who had overcome his own obstacles
(C) the author was a genuine fan of Heller's most famous book
(D) the author had been so unimpressed by Heller's speech at his high school
(E) Heller had taken the time to come to visit a high school, even though he was a celebrity

1	A	B	C	D	E
2	A	B	C	D	E
3	A	B	C	D	E
4	A	B	C	D	E
5	A	B	C	D	E
6	A	B	C	D	E

Answers and Explanations: Practice Passage 4

1 *D* This is the first question—which makes it likely that we will find the answer in the first paragraph. Was the book "little-known" as choice A says? No, according to the author it was famous, and "an anthem" for the author and his friends. Was the book about high school students, as choice B suggests? No, according to the author it was about a soldier during World War II. Was the book too traditional, as choice C suggests? From the description offered in paragraph 2, this was not a traditional book. Traditional books have heroes, not anti-heroes. Inspiring and thoughtful, as choice D suggests? Yes, and note that the answer came from the first paragraph. Let's hold onto this one. Was the book more suited to an older generation, as choice E suggests? These kids seemed to like it just fine. The best answer is choice D.

2 *A* You probably had a good idea of the answer to this general question by the time you'd finished the other questions. Was this a profile of Joseph Heller? Of course not. It was mostly about one incident in which the writer of this passage saw and met Heller. Scratch choice B. Choice C might have been tempting but for the word "early" and the "s" on the end of "memories." This passage concerned one memory, and it did not concern the author's early childhood. Choice D reflected a momentary disappointment the author felt, but by the end of the passage he was clearly over it. While the passage does fleetingly describe *Catch-22*, it is mostly devoted to describing the day of Heller's appearance at the school. The best answer is choice A.

3 *D* To answer this EXCEPT question, we have to read a little above and below the quoted lines to find out how this sentence fits the context of the entire paragraph. The writer had expected Heller to make the big entrance of a famous person, but instead he just walked up by himself. This tells us something about: A, the difference between the writer's picture of Heller and the reality; B, the normal way in which Heller chose to live his life; C, how the writer of the passage was thinking; and E, the age of the sneakers themselves. However, it does not suggest that Heller had dressed like this just to make an impression on his audience. The best answer is choice D.

4 *D* Choice A was tempting here, because clearly by the end of the speech, the wit and imagery of the novelist had captured his audience. However, the purpose of the paragraph was to illustrate the fact that the audience was captured, which makes choice D the best answer. Likewise, choices B and E accurately describe how the students first reacted to Heller, but by the end of the speech, they had changed their minds. Choice C says this paragraph was to respond to charges against Heller's works, but no such charges are made in the passage.

5 *C* The expression "to field a question" probably has its roots in baseball, where you "field" a hit, but the sense of the word in this case was simply "responded to." There was no reason to suppose that Heller was on the defensive and had to "evade" questions, or that he was so caught up in the questions that he had to "delve" (meaning "go deeper") into them. The best answer is choice C.

6 *B* Let's get rid of the impossible answer choices. Choice A does not seem like enough of a reason to remember a handshake. Choice D was wrong because the author of the passage ended up being very impressed by Heller. Choice E seems a bit too generic to be the reason the author would remember a handshake from someone he clearly admired a lot. We're down between choices B and C. Was it just because he liked Heller's work, or had he been somehow touched by something deeper? The best answer is choice B.

CRITICAL READING: PRACTICE PASSAGE 5

Using the information contained in the passage and introductory material below, answer the questions that follow.

Recommended time: about 8 minutes

Questions 1-9 are based on the following passage.

This passage describes the first detailed observations of the surface of the planet Mars—observations that indirectly led some to the mistaken belief that intelligent life existed there.

The summer of 1877 had been an exceptional time for observing Mars. Every 26 months the slower-moving Mars comes especially close to Earth, creating the most favorable opportunity for observations—or, in the space age, for travel to the planet. Sometimes these opportunities are better than others. Because of the large ellipticy* of the Martian orbit, the distance between Mars and Earth at the closest approach of opposition (when Mars is on the opposite side of Earth from the Sun) varies from as near as 35 million miles to as far as 63 million. The closest of these oppositions occurs approximately every 15 years, and 1877 was one of those choice viewing times.

Among the astronomers taking advantage of the opportunity was Giovani Virginio Schiaparelli, director of the Milan Observatory and a scientist highly esteemed, particularly for his research concerning meteors and comets. While examining Mars with a relatively small 8-inch telescope, Schiaparelli saw faint linear markings across the disc. Earlier observers had glimpsed some such streaks, but nothing as prominent and widespread as those Schiaparelli described seeing. His drawings of Mars showed the dark areas, which some took to be seas, connected by an extensive network of long straight lines. Schiaparelli called the lines *canali*.

In Italian, the primary meaning of *canali* is "channels" or "grooves," which is presumably what Schiaparelli intended in the initial announcement of his discovery. He said that they "may be designated as *canali* although we do not yet know what they are." But the word can also mean "canal," which is how it usually was translated. The difference in meanings had tremendous theoretical implications.

"The whole hypothesis was right there in the translation," science writer Carl Sagan has said. "Somebody saw canals on Mars. Well, what does that mean? Well, canal—everybody knows what a canal is. How do you get a canal? Somebody builds it. Well, then there are *builders* of canals on Mars."

It may be no coincidence that the Martian canals inspired extravagant speculation at a time when canal building on Earth was a reigning symbol of the Age of Progress. The Suez Canal was completed in 1869, and the first efforts to breach Central America at Nicaragua or Panama were being promoted. To cut through miles of land and join two seas, to mold imperfect nature to suit man—in the nineteenth-century way of thinking, this was surely how intelligent beings met challenges, whether on Earth or on Mars.

Schiaparelli seemed to be of two minds about the markings. Of the canal-builders' interpretation he once remarked, "I am careful not to combat this suggestion, which contains nothing impossible." But he would not encourage speculation. At another time, Schiaparelli elaborated on observations suggesting to him that the snows and ice of the Martian north pole were associated with the canals. When snows are melting with the change of season, the breadth of the canals increases and temporary seas appear, he noted, and in the winter the canals diminish and some of the seas disappear. But he saw a thoroughly natural explanation for the canals. "It is not necessary to suppose them to be the work of intelligent beings," he wrote in 1893, "and notwithstanding the almost geometrical appearance of all of their system, we are now inclined to believe them to be produced by the evolution of the planet, just as on the Earth we have the English Channel."

His cautionary words had little effect. Those who wanted to believe in a system of water canals on Mars, built by intelligent beings, were not to be discouraged—or proven wrong—for another 70 years.

* *Ellipticy* refers to an oval (rather than a perfectly round) orbit around the sun.

1 Which of the following dates was likely to be the best for viewing Mars?

(A) 6 months prior to the summer of 1877
(B) 26 months after the summer of 1877
(C) 15 years after the summer of 1877
(D) 26 months before the summer of 1877
(E) 1 month prior to the summer of 1877

2 In line 18, the word "choice" means most nearly

(A) accepted
(B) optional
(C) exclusive
(D) preferred
(E) selected

3 According to the author, which best indicates the definition of "*canali*" (line 37) that Schiaparelli most likely originally intended?

(A) extensive networks
(B) dark sea-like areas
(C) channels or grooves
(D) long canals
(E) moon-like deserts

4 The author quotes Carl Sagan in lines 47-54, primarily to

(A) introduce another modern writer's views into his discussion
(B) illustrate the thought process that led to a misunderstanding
(C) discuss the feasibility of building canals on Mars
(D) discount the theories of Schiaparelli
(E) reveal that the sightings of the canali were unsubstantiated and incorrect

5 Which statement best summarizes the point made in the fifth paragraph?

(A) The sightings of the Mars canals in 1877 led to a surge of canal building on Earth.
(B) The readiness to believe that the *canali* were constructed by intelligent beings may have come from a general fascination with canal building at the time.
(C) The Suez Canal's completion in 1869 set in motion another canal-building project which ultimately became the Panama Canal.
(D) Canal building is one important way to measure the relative intelligence and development of civilizations.
(E) Differences in the meaning of the word "*canali*" caused imperfections in the efforts to join two seas in Central America

6 The author's tone in using the words, "surely how intelligent beings . . . on Mars" (lines 66-68) is meant to express

(A) irony
(B) despair
(C) uncertainty
(D) rage
(E) apathy

7 In line 69, "of two minds" means

(A) undecided
(B) tentative
(C) changeable
(D) vague
(E) skeptical

8 To what did Schiaparelli attribute the periodic changes in the appearance of the Martian canals described in the sixth paragraph?

(A) The ellipticy of the Martian orbit exerts a tidal pull on the water in the canals.
(B) The visual distortion of Schiaparelli's relatively small telescope caused the image to change.
(C) Changes in the distance between the Earth and Mars make objects appear to get smaller or larger.
(D) The canals get inundated by temporary seas.
(E) Melted ice from the north pole flows into the canals during some seasons, enlarging them.

9 According to the author, what did Schiaparelli ultimately decide about the *canali* he had discovered?

(A) The *canali* showed that life on Mars is not impossible.
(B) Their geometrical appearance was misstated: The canals did not exist as straight lines, but as curves.
(C) They were most likely a phenomena created by nature.
(D) The canals evolved from less intelligent life.
(E) They were constructed to provide irrigation to lands far away from the seas.

1 ⊂A⊃ ⊂B⊃ ⊂C⊃ ⊂D⊃ ⊂E⊃
2 ⊂A⊃ ⊂B⊃ ⊂C⊃ ⊂D⊃ ⊂E⊃
3 ⊂A⊃ ⊂B⊃ ⊂C⊃ ⊂D⊃ ⊂E⊃
4 ⊂A⊃ ⊂B⊃ ⊂C⊃ ⊂D⊃ ⊂E⊃
5 ⊂A⊃ ⊂B⊃ ⊂C⊃ ⊂D⊃ ⊂E⊃
6 ⊂A⊃ ⊂B⊃ ⊂C⊃ ⊂D⊃ ⊂E⊃
7 ⊂A⊃ ⊂B⊃ ⊂C⊃ ⊂D⊃ ⊂E⊃
8 ⊂A⊃ ⊂B⊃ ⊂C⊃ ⊂D⊃ ⊂E⊃
9 ⊂A⊃ ⊂B⊃ ⊂C⊃ ⊂D⊃ ⊂E⊃

Answers and Explanations: Practice Passage 5

1 *C* The answer to this first question was, as you might imagine, in the first paragraph. The summer of 1877 had been one of the best times for viewing Mars. According to the passage, every 26 months there was another good opportunity to view Mars, but the best time to observe the planet was every 15 years. Thus, the best answer is in some increment of 15 years before or after the summer of 1877. The best answer is choice C.

2 *D* The "choice viewing time" the author is talking about in the quoted line is one of the occasions we were just referring to in the explanation to question 1, when the Earth and Mars are closest and can be most easily viewed with a telescope. In this context, the best definition offered is choice D, "preferred."

3 *C* Rereading from the beginning of the third paragraph, ". . . the primary meaning of *canali* is "channels" or "grooves," which is presumably what Schiaparelli intended . . ." Well, that's enough for us! The best answer is choice C.

4 *B* Sagan does not discuss whether or not the hypothesis was true, or the feasibility of building canals on Mars, nor does he make fun of Schaparelli, or discredit the sightings of the canali. He merely illustrates how the people at that time reached the conclusion that there might be intelligent life on Mars. The best answer is choice B. Choice A is just kind of odd; would the author mention a modern writer for no real reason?

5 *B* Choice A gets the chain of events backward. The Suez canal was finished in 1869—well before the *canali* were spotted on Mars. The canal across Panama was mentioned in the passage, but it certainly wasn't the main idea of the paragraph—so we can rule out both choices C and E. It may be that at the time people thought canal-building represented higher intelligence, but once again this was not the main idea of the paragraph, so we can eliminate choice D.

The best answer is choice B. Because canal building was trendy at the time on Earth, it made people more interested—and more willing to believe—in the so-called canals on Mars.

6 *A* This part of the passage gently mocks the nineteenth-century people who thought canal building was the highest possible pinnacle of intellectual progress. The best answer was choice A, "irony." If you weren't sure about the correct answer, you could still have eliminated several choices because they were almost ridiculous. Reading this paragraph, did you think the tone was that of despair, rage, or apathy? These were easy eliminations.

7 *A* In the context of this sentence, Schiaparelli's being "of two minds" did not mean he was changing his mind every five minutes ("changeable"), or that he didn't believe in either of the two theories ("skeptical"), or that he was indistinct or blurred ("vague"), or that he was feeling experimental ("tentative"). The best answer here is that he was A, "undecided."

8 *E* Where did Schiaparelli describe the changes in the canals? That's right: the second to last paragraph. In lines 76-84, he spoke of "observations suggesting to him that the snows and ice of the Martian north pole were associated with the canals. When snows are melting . . . the breadth of the canals increases." Choice D might have seemed tempting because the temporary seas are mentioned here, but the passage does not say that the seas swallow up the canals. The best answer is choice E.

9 *C* This is the last question, so the answer will probably be found toward the end of the passage. In lines 84-86, the author writes, "But he saw a thoroughly natural explanation for the canals," and then the author quotes Schiaparelli saying, ". . . we are now inclined to believe [the canals] to be produced by the evolution of the planet . . ." The best answer is choice C.

CRITICAL READING: PRACTICE PASSAGE 6

Using the information contained in the passage and introductory material below, answer the questions that follow.

Recommended time: about 7 minutes

Questions 1-6 are based on the following passage.

In the following excerpt from a novel, Pearl, an elderly woman, is speaking to her son.

Pearl opened her eyes when Ezra turned a page of his magazine. "Ezra," she said. She felt him grow still. He had this habit—he had always had it—of becoming totally motionless when people spoke to him. It was endearing but also in some ways a strain, for then whatever she said to him ("I feel a draft," or "the paper boy is late again") was bound to disappoint him, wasn't it? How could she live up to Ezra's expectations? She plucked at her quilt. "If I could just have some water," she told him.

He poured it from the pitcher on the bureau. She heard no ice cubes clinking; they must have melted. Yet it seemed just minutes ago that he'd brought in a whole new supply. He raised her head, rested it on his shoulder, and tipped the glass to her lips. Yes, lukewarm—not that she minded. She drank gratefully, keeping her eyes closed. His shoulder felt steady and comforting. He laid her back down on the pillow.

"Dr. Vincent's coming at ten," he told her.

"What time is it now?"

"Eight-thirty."

"Eight-thirty in the morning?"

"Yes."

"Have you been here all night?" she asked.

"I slept a little."

"Sleep now. I won't be needing you."

"Well, maybe after the doctor comes."

It was important to Pearl that she deceive the doctor. She didn't want to go to the hospital. Her illness was pneumonia, she was almost certain; she guessed it from a past experience. She recognized the way it settled into her back. If Dr. Vincent found out he would take her out of her own bed, her own house, and send her off to Union Memorial, tent her over with plastic. "Maybe you should cancel the doctor altogether," she told Ezra. "I'm very much improved, I believe."

"Let him decide that."

"Well, I know how my own self feels, Ezra."

"We won't argue about it just now," he said.

He could surprise you, Ezra could. He'd let a person walk all over him but then display, at odd moments, a deep and rock-hard stubbornness. She sighed and smoothed her quilt. Wasn't it supposed to be the daughter who came and nursed you? She knew she should send him away but she couldn't make herself do it. "I guess you want to get back to that restaurant," she told him.

"No, no."

"You're like a mother hen about that place," she said. She sniffed. Then she said, "Ezra, do you smell smoke?"

Why do you ask?" he said (cautious as ever).

"I dreamed the house burned down."

"It didn't really."

"Ah."

She waited, holding herself in. Her muscles were so tense, she ached all over. Finally she said, "Ezra?"

"Yes Mother?"

"Maybe you could just check."

"Check what?"

"The house, of course. Check if it's on fire."

1 How does the author reveal the passage of time in the second paragraph?

(A) The sun has just come up.
(B) The ice cubes in the pitcher have melted.
(C) Ezra has finally arrived.
(D) Pearl closes her eyes and dreams.
(E) The water in the pitcher is cold.

2 It can be inferred from the dialogue in lines 25-35 that Pearl has spent the night

(A) talking to Ezra about the past
(B) making plans to go to the hospital
(C) talking on the telephone to her friends
(D) sleeping in her bed
(E) worrying about the future

3 If Ezra knew that Pearl had pneumonia, he would most probably

(A) agree to let her stay where she is
(B) insist that she go to the hospital
(C) make sure that she gets more rest and drinks fluids
(D) agree to lie to the doctor about her illness in order to help his mother stay out of the hospital
(E) ask another doctor for a second opinion

4 The passage suggests that in this scene Pearl is

(A) in the hospital
(B) staying with Ezra at his house
(C) living at home
(D) living in a hotel
(E) at a health clinic

5 The author writes, " She sighed and smoothed her quilt," (lines 57-58) in order to convey that Pearl

(A) is exasperated with her son and wishes he would leave her alone
(B) is tired and wishes to sleep
(C) has given up trying to persuade Ezra to cancel the doctor
(D) is a fastidious person who dislikes wrinkled things
(E) is no longer completely in touch with reality

6 The passage suggests that Pearl's fears that the house is on fire

(A) are likely to turn out to be true
(B) have no basis whatsoever
(C) came as a result of a dream she had
(D) are just a way to get her son to leave her alone for a moment
(E) are the result of a sleepless night

1 ⊂A⊃ ⊂B⊃ ⊂C⊃ ⊂D⊃ ⊂E⊃
2 ⊂A⊃ ⊂B⊃ ⊂C⊃ ⊂D⊃ ⊂E⊃
3 ⊂A⊃ ⊂B⊃ ⊂C⊃ ⊂D⊃ ⊂E⊃
4 ⊂A⊃ ⊂B⊃ ⊂C⊃ ⊂D⊃ ⊂E⊃
5 ⊂A⊃ ⊂B⊃ ⊂C⊃ ⊂D⊃ ⊂E⊃
6 ⊂A⊃ ⊂B⊃ ⊂C⊃ ⊂D⊃ ⊂E⊃

Answers and Explanations: Practice Passage 6

1 *B* Go back to the second paragraph and read it again. How do we know from this paragraph that time has gone by? Let's go through the answer choices and do a little elimination. The second paragraph doesn't mention that the sun has come up. Later in the passage, Ezra tells Pearl it is already morning, but he hasn't told her this by the second paragraph. Eliminate choice A. Choice B seems very possible. If Pearl feels that Ezra brought ice only a few minutes ago, and yet the ice has melted, that implies that she has missed some time. Let's hold on to that one. Choice C is wrong because Ezra has been present all night. Eliminate C. Pearl does close her eyes in this passage, but only while she is drinking. It's hard to see the passage of time in a sip of water, so choice D bites the dust. Choice E directly contradicts the passage: The water is not cold—it is now lukewarm. The correct answer must be choice B.

2 *D* At no time in this passage is the answer to this question stated directly. However, there are a series of clues. First, Pearl opens her eyes at the beginning. Second, the ice cubes that Ezra had brought "it seemed just minutes ago" were already melted. And third, she doesn't know whether it is day or night. What has she been doing? That's right: getting some z's. The best answer is choice D.

3 *B* This question has no line number, but it's easy to find the lead word "pneumonia" in line 39.

If Ezra knew Pearl had pneumonia, what would he do about it? This is a hypothetical question. To answer it, we must think about what we know of Ezra. He stayed with Pearl all night. When she drank some water, he propped her up with his own shoulder. And he refused to go to sleep until after he'd heard what the doctor had to say. Given all this, what do you think he would do if he knew she had pneumonia? The best answer is choice B.

4 *C* Again, there is no line number, but the answer to question 4 is likely to come right after the answer to question 3.

When you first started the passage, you may have leapt to the conclusion that she was in the hospital already. However, there is one key place in the passage where we find out exactly where she is: lines 42-45. Here, directly stated, is her intention to try to avoid going to the hospital (meaning she isn't there now) and her intention to stay in "her own bed, her own house." The only possible answer is choice C.

5 *C* As always, you should read a little bit above and below the cited line to understand the context of the quoted words. Pearl has been trying to persuade Ezra not to let the doctor come, but he has been stubborn and without actually saying no, has indicated he will not cancel the doctor's visit. Choices B, D and E do not seem to have anything to do with what has just happened. Both choices A and C could be legitimate reactions to Ezra's refusal to let her have her way. But "sighing" seems more a sign of resignation than of anger. The best answer is choice C.

6 *C* There is no real indication that the house is actually on fire, so we can eliminate choice A, but Pearl's fears are not based on nothing—she has had a dream. Thus, we can eliminate choice B, and the best answer is choice C. Choice D is theoretically possible, but not supported by the text. Choice E is contradicted by the fact that Pearl has been dreaming.

CRITICAL READING: PRACTICE PASSAGE 7

Using the information contained in the two passages and the introductory material below, answer the questions that follow.

Recommended time: 15 minutes

Questions 1-12 are based on the following passages.

The following two passages present two views of the funeral industry in the United States. The first passage is an excerpt from a book written in 1963 by a journalist, and takes a hard look at funeral practices at the time. The second passage was written in the 1980s by a member of the funeral business and looks at the changes in the industry since the first book appeared.

Passage I

Oh death, where is thy sting? O grave, where is thy victory? Where, indeed. Many a badly stung survivor faced with the aftermath of some relative's funeral, has ruefully concluded that the victory has been won hands down by a funeral establishment—in disastrously unequal battle.

Much has been written of late about the affluent society in which we live, and much fun poked at some of the irrational "status symbols" set out like golden snares to trap the unwary consumer at every turn. Until recently, little has been said about the most irrational and weirdest of the lot, lying in ambush for all of us at the end of the road—the modern American funeral.

If the dismal traders (as an eighteenth-century English writer calls them) have traditionally been cast in a comic role in literature, a universally recognized symbol of humor from Shakespeare to Dickens to Evelyn Waugh, they have successfully turned the tables in recent years to perpetrate a huge, macabre and expensive practical joke on the American public. It is not consciously conceived of as a joke, of course; on the contrary, it is hedged with admirably contrived rationalizations.

Gradually, almost imperceptibly, over the years, the funeral men have constructed their own grotesque cloud-cuckoo-land where the trappings of Gracious Living are transformed, as in a nightmare, into the trappings of Gracious Dying. The same familiar Madison Avenue language has seeped into the funeral industry.

So that this too, too solid flesh might not melt, we are offered "solid copper—a quality casket which offers superb value to the client seeking long-lasting protection," or the "colonial Classic Beauty—18 gauge lead-coated steel, seamless top, lap-jointed welded body construction." Some caskets are equipped with foam rubber, some with innerspring mattresses. One company actually offers "the revolutionary Perfect-Posture bed."

Passage II

In the past twenty years, many of the questionable excesses of the funeral trade have been curbed: Legislation and self-policing by funeral home associations have brought some measure of regulation to an industry that was at one time sadly deficient. And yet, if the sharp practices of shoddy morticians are no longer cause for customers to "whirl in their urns," as Jessica Mitford once put it so trenchantly, I fear that we may have somehow tilted too far in the other direction.

True, the costs of funerals in the 1960s were escalating out of all proportion to real value, but I am convinced that in our search for economy and avoidance of discomfort we have weakened a very important family rite. Consider the case of one funeral "park" in Southern California that has instituted "drive-in" funerals. Believe it or not, you can view the remains, attend the chapel service, and witness the interment—all without leaving your car.

To the extent that measures such as these have cut costs, I would applaud, but in my opinion these measures have also produced a disconnection from the real purposes of a funeral. The process of spending time mourning the dead fills a real need for the bereaved. There is a purpose to each of the steps of a funeral, and if there is a commensurate cost to those steps, then so be it. These days it is possible to have a funeral without a service for friends and family to gather, without a graveside interment, even without a casket. More frequently now, families will ask that contributions to charity be made in lieu of flowers and wreaths—without recognizing that buying flowers provides a chance for friends and relatives to show their concern in a more tangible way than a gift to charity.

Let us not forget that feelings are as important as economy.

1 Why does the author of the first passage use the quote, "O, death, where is thy sting?" (line 1)

(A) to introduce the subject of death in a literary fashion
(B) as a quick way to get people's attention
(C) to suggest that the sting of death can also affect the living who must pay for the funeral
(D) to illustrate that funeral directors are caring members of a sensitive profession
(E) to suggest that death has no affect on the author of this passage

2 According to the passage, the "dismal traders" mentioned in line 19, are

(A) undertakers
(B) shopkeepers
(C) writers such as Shakespeare and Dickens
(D) practical jokers
(E) stock and bond salesmen

3 According to the fourth and fifth paragraph of the first passage, to sell their new products, funeral directors are using

(A) free consultation and advice sessions
(B) incentive plans designed to get customers to purchase funerals while they are still alive
(C) the language of advertising
(D) family specials
(E) young spokespersons who are skilled at sales tactics

4 The tone of the first passage's author could best be described as

(A) nostalgic
(B) ironic
(C) happy
(D) indifferent
(E) lyrical

5 If the author of the first passage were to plan her funeral in advance, which of the following would she most likely try to do?

(A) buy an expensive casket with a Perfect Posture mattress inside
(B) invite her friends to a service at a funeral home
(C) buy a burial plot overlooking a river
(D) prepay her funeral so that it could be as elaborate as possible
(E) leave instructions for a simple, inexpensive funeral

6 In line 55 of the second passage, the word "curbed" most nearly means

(A) brought under control
(B) kept under wraps
(C) led aside
(D) established
(E) kept at a constant level

7 According to the second passage, the excesses of the funeral trade have been changed for the better as a result of

(A) the passage of time
(B) the institution of services such as drive-in funerals
(C) the elimination of flowers and wreaths at services
(D) new government laws and trade association rules
(E) the practices of shoddy morticians

8 The author cites the example of the "drive-in funeral" (lines 72-73) in order to

(A) illustrate the point that such practices take away from the real purposes of a funeral
(B) condemn the people who consent to mourn in this way
(C) demonstrate the ways in which the funeral industry has changed for the better
(D) respond to charges that the industry is still sadly deficient
(E) rebut claims that the industry has failed to change in the past twenty years

9 The phrase "in lieu of" (line 92) most nearly means

(A) as well as
(B) because of
(C) instead of
(D) in addition to
(E) on the side of

10 The contrast between the two descriptions of the funeral industry is essentially one between

(A) rank pessimism and new-found dread
(B) greedy opportunism and mature professionalism
(C) uncertain pride and unsure self-esteem
(D) jealous warnings and alert alarms
(E) lawless exhaustion and tireless energy

11 Both authors indicate that the funeral industry

(A) continues to engage in shoddy practices
(B) fulfills a real need in the community
(C) can police itself
(D) preys on the suffering of the bereaved
(E) was in a troubled state in the 1960s

12 The contrast between the two passages reflects primarily the biases of

(A) an older woman and a younger man
(B) a native of the United States and a native of Europe
(C) an optimist and a pessimist
(D) an investigative journalist and a member of the funeral industry
(E) a person from the east coast, and a person from the west coast

1 ⊂A⊃ ⊂B⊃ ⊂C⊃ ⊂D⊃ ⊂E⊃
2 ⊂A⊃ ⊂B⊃ ⊂C⊃ ⊂D⊃ ⊂E⊃
3 ⊂A⊃ ⊂B⊃ ⊂C⊃ ⊂D⊃ ⊂E⊃
4 ⊂A⊃ ⊂B⊃ ⊂C⊃ ⊂D⊃ ⊂E⊃
5 ⊂A⊃ ⊂B⊃ ⊂C⊃ ⊂D⊃ ⊂E⊃
6 ⊂A⊃ ⊂B⊃ ⊂C⊃ ⊂D⊃ ⊂E⊃
7 ⊂A⊃ ⊂B⊃ ⊂C⊃ ⊂D⊃ ⊂E⊃
8 ⊂A⊃ ⊂B⊃ ⊂C⊃ ⊂D⊃ ⊂E⊃
9 ⊂A⊃ ⊂B⊃ ⊂C⊃ ⊂D⊃ ⊂E⊃
10 ⊂A⊃ ⊂B⊃ ⊂C⊃ ⊂D⊃ ⊂E⊃
11 ⊂A⊃ ⊂B⊃ ⊂C⊃ ⊂D⊃ ⊂E⊃
12 ⊂A⊃ ⊂B⊃ ⊂C⊃ ⊂D⊃ ⊂E⊃

Answers and Explanations: Practice Passage 7

1 *C* Reading just a little further past the cited lines, it becomes clear that the author thinks that one of death's stings these days is the bill relatives have to pay for the funeral. While you could make an argument for both choices A and B, choice C is the best answer.

2 *A* This question is a bit difficult. The author does not spell out her meaning here, but the entire passage is about the funeral industry, so it is a logical inference that the "dismal traders" are, in fact, undertakers. While Dickens and Shakespeare are mentioned in the paragraph, it is fairly clear from the context that they are not the "dismal traders." Similarly, while the passage says the dismal traders have perpetrated a practical joke, it also says that this joke is not "consciously conceived of as a joke," and thus it seems incorrect to call them practical jokers. The best answer is choice A.

3 *C* It is in the fourth and fifth paragraphs that the author talks about new funeral products. In those paragraphs she says that the funeral industry uses the vocabulary of "Madison Avenue"—a common reference to the advertising industry. She also quotes the industry's jargon to describe their products, and the jargon sounds just like the phrases you would read in an advertisement for a new car.

4 *B* The author is certainly making fun of the funeral industry, mocking their language and their practices. Her tone is not nostalgic, happy, indifferent, or lyrical. It is ironic, choice B.

5 *E* After reading the passage it is clear that the author detests expensive, overblown funerals. The best answer is choice E.

6 *A* The key to this vocabulary question came in the same sentence as the key to question 6: "The excesses...have been curbed" by legislation, etc., that "have brought some measure of regulation...to the industry." Effectively, "curbed" means to bring excesses under regulation. Which answer choices are close to this meaning? The only two possibilities are choices A and E. Now, does the author mean that the "questionable excesses" of the funeral industry have been brought under control or kept at a constant level? Since it's clear she believes the situation has improved, the best answer choice is A.

7 *D* The answer to this question can be found in the first paragraph of the second passage, right after the colon in the first sentence: "...legislation and self-policing by funeral home associations have brought some measure of regulation...." Thus the best answer is choice D. Choices B and C, while economies that might help customers, are not broad enough to stop the excesses of an entire industry.

8 *A* The example of the "drive-in" is introduced with the words, "Consider the case of..." Obviously this is meant to be an example to illustrate a point that was just made: "...that in our search for economy and avoidance of discomfort, we have weakened a very important family rite." Which answer choice resembles this sentiment? If you said choice A, you were absolutely right. Choice B is tempting because the author does seem to be condemning drive-in funerals, but the point of the example is not to make fun of the people who attend, but to point out an important feature that these funerals lack.

9 *C* If you weren't sure what "in lieu of" meant, the second half of the sentence might help. Here, the author makes it clear that if a contribution has been made "in lieu of" flowers, then the contributors have not bought the flowers. This means we can get rid of choices A, D, and E. Substituting "because of" for "in lieu of" does not produce an understandable sentence. Hence, the best answer is choice C.

10 *B* The first passage paints a bleak view of an industry run amok—overcharging customers left and right. The second passage portrays a more mature, self-policing industry. The best answer is choice B. Since we know from the introductory material that the two passages are presenting at least slightly differing opinions on the same subject, it is easy to eliminate choices A and C, which do not offer contrasting visions of the industry.

11 *E* The second passage maintains that the funeral industry is much better than it used to be, which means we can eliminate choices A and D. The first passage would disagree with choices B and C, allowing us to eliminate them as well.

The introductory material was crucial to understanding the answer to this question. The first passage was written during the 1960s and detailed the harmful practices of the funeral trade. The second passage was written during the 1980s and looked back 20 years to the same harmful practices. The best answer is choice E.

12 *D* The answer to this question is also found in the introductory blurb. The ages, nationalities, and regions of the two writers were not discussed, so we can eliminate choices A, B, and E. While you may have felt the first passage was written by a pessimist and the second by an optimist, choice D is slightly better than choice C.

5

Vocabulary

VOCABULARY

From a long-term perspective, the best way to improve your vocabulary is to read. Some teachers and vocabulary books will tell you to read the classics or scholarly journals, but if you aren't interested in these things, then reading will be painful and unpleasant, and you won't end up doing it.

Instead, think of a subject that totally fascinates you. It could be anything: the history of comic books; detective novels; sports; true romance; or a popular movie star. Believe it or not, there will be at least one book available in your library or bookstore on any subject you can think of.

Your English teacher may be horrified, but reading anything will get you into the habit of reading, as well as exposing you to new words.

Of course, you won't know what those words mean unless you look them up. The test-writers at ETS use two dictionaries as they assemble words for the SAT: *The American Heritage Dictionary* and *Webster's New Collegiate Dictionary*. We recommend that you buy one of these; you'll need a good dictionary in college anyway. As you read, get in the habit of looking up words you don't know. It's easy to slide over an unfamiliar word, particularly if you understand the rest of the sentence it's in. However, even if you can figure out the author's meaning, make it a point to look up the word.

Some students like to keep a small notebook and pen next to their dictionary. Whenever they look up a word, they write it down in the notebook along with a two- or three-word definition. Later they can quiz themselves on the words.

USING THE WORDS YOU KNOW

Research has shown that the most effective way to memorize anything is to use it in some organic way. For example, if you wanted to memorize a recipe for baked chicken, the most effective way to do it would be to cook the recipe several times. If you wanted to memorize your lines for a school play, the best way to do it would be to say your lines out loud a few times with a friend. Probably the least effective way to memorize anything is to stare at it on the printed page.

The best way to remember words is to use them frequently in conversation. You may feel a little self-conscious the first couple of times you try this, but as you get used to it, you will become more brazen. It's actually pretty easy to find an excuse to use new vocabulary words in almost any situation.

For example, here's a word from our Hit Parade, chosen at random: "erratic" (meaning "unpredictably eccentric") and a situation, also chosen at random: you are trying to explain to a parent why you didn't get a good grade on a history test. Here are three ways to use the word:

"Mom, I'm sorry my performance has been a little erratic lately." (Playing for sympathy, but also designed to impress her with an adult-sounding word.)

"My history teacher is just so erratic that I don't know what to study. Last time he tested only material from the class, but this time he tested stuff out of the textbook that we never even talked about." (Don't blame me, it's all the fault of my psychotic history teacher.)

"Dad, I must say I find your concern to be erratic at best. If you wanted me to study for this test, you shouldn't have let me watch television all weekend. (The best defense is a good offense.)

THE HIT PARADE

Whether you have a year or a week to prepare for the verbal SAT, the best way to start is to learn the words that are most likely to show up on the test. We've taken around 250 of the most often-used words on the SAT and put them together in this chapter. You may be surprised at how many of these words you already know. The SAT does not test esoteric words such as esurient. Instead, you will find words that a college freshman is likely to need to know (for example: "esoteric." Have you looked it up yet?).

Bearing in mind that the best way to learn words is to use them in conversation, we have organized the words around common situations in which you might find yourself. If you are going to be eating dinner with your family, read our "At the Dinner Table" section first and then try out a few words on your unsuspecting family. If you are going to a basketball game after school, read our section "At the Game" and then casually drop a few Hit Parade words into your color commentary.

Even if one of our "common" situations does not seem pertinent to you—"On Trial For Your Life" comes to mind—make it a point to learn the words anyway. Time has shown that ETS uses these words frequently.

If you find you can't work all these words into your conversation, there are two other great ways to memorize words.

MNEMONICS

Many students find that they remember words best if they come up with images to help them remember. These images are known as mnemonics. For example, one of the students in our SAT course wanted to remember the meaning of hiatus ("a break or lapse in continuity").

So whenever she sees that word she pretends she's addressing a friend,

> "Hi, (long pause) Atus."

Another student in our SAT course wanted to remember the meaning of the word abridge ("to shorten"). Whenever he sees the word, he thinks,

"A shrt brdge."

It doesn't matter how silly or bizarre your image is, as long as you won't forget it.

FLASHCARDS

Just as running lines will help you to memorize your part in a production of *Death of a Salesman*, going over the words on the Hit Parade again and again will help you to commit them to memory. A good way to accomplish this is to write down the words you want to remember—in a notebook or, even better, on flashcards. Put the word on one side of the card, and the definition on the other. By carrying the flashcards around with you, you can quiz yourself in spare moments—riding home from school, or waiting for class to begin.

To help you get started, we have bound into this book a set of flash cards complete with Hit Parade words on one side and definitions on the other.

A FINAL WORD

No matter how much you practice the techniques in the other sections of this book, you will not substantially improve your verbal score without learning additional vocabulary. The Hit Parade that follows is hopefully only the beginning.

Almost nothing else that you can do will change people's perception of you as much as using a more erudite vocabulary. It's more effective than plastic surgery, and much less expensive.

THE HIT PARADE

At the Dinner Table

I **abhor** lima beans; they taste awful to me.

Would it be **presumptuous** of me to ask for seconds?

Your **subtle** use of seasonings was just right.

Hey! Don't **hoard** the mashed potatoes at your end of the table.

I think this rib roast is **tainted**; don't eat it!

On a Diet

No more for me. I'm being **abstemious**.

I'm totally **satiated**. I couldn't eat another bite.

I'm feeling **replete**. No more mashed potatoes for me.

No thanks, more food would be **superfluous**.

No more brussels sprouts; my plate has reached a **plateau**.

I've already had a **surfeit** of dinner. No more, please.

abhor	to loathe or detest
abstemious	sparing in the use of food or drink
hoard	to accumulate or stash away
plateau	a condition of neither growth nor decline
presumptuous	bold to the point of rudeness
replete	gorged with food, sated
satiate	satisfy fully
subtle	hardly noticeable
superfluous	unnecessary
surfeit	excess, overindulgence
taint	to affect with something harmful; contaminate

"What Do You Want to Do?" "I Don't Know, What Do You Want to Do?"

(With these words, you can take indecision to new heights.)

I'm **vacillating** between going to a movie or going to the mall. What about you?

I'm completely **apathetic**. I'll do whatever you want to do.

Well I'm **indifferent** too. I'll do whatever you want to do.

Maybe since we're feeling so **ambiguous**, we should just hang out here.

No, my mental state is too **precarious** to just stay here.

If you're **skeptical** about your mental health then maybe we should just skip it.

ambiguous	unclear, having more than one meaning
apathy	lack of interest or caring
indifference	lack of interest, feeling or opinion
precarious	unstable, insecure
skeptical	showing doubt and disbelief
vacillation	wavering, going back and forth

Shopping

I have a **penchant** for blue suede shoes; I can't have enough!

I have such a **paucity** of clothes that I barely have anything to wear.

Dad, you are such a **philanthropist** with your donations to my shopping funds.

I know you may believe I'm being **prodigal**, but I really need this CD-ROM player.

Do you think I would be a **spendthrift** if I bought this $100 shirt?

I think this blouse has a lot of **utility**—it goes with everything I own!

This shirt is very **versatile**—you can wear it inside-out too!

paucity	small amount or number
penchant	a strong taste or liking
philanthropist	someone who gives to worthy causes
prodigal	wasteful
spendthrift	a person who spends money wastefully
utility	usefulness
versatile	capable of doing many things well

Strong Words

Kim was known for her honesty and **integrity**, and would never **exploit** someone's weaknesses to her advantage.

John knew how hard it was to be a beginner, so he was always ready to teach a **novice**. For this, his friends **revered** him.

Selena had a **yearning** to write a 1000-page novel, and nothing less would **satiate** her. Sadly, the school newspaper could only print a few hundred words, so she had to **truncate** her story considerably.

Though he tried to resist, Larry **succumbed** to his desire for a triple-chocolate fudge sundae.

After the politician was accused of **slander**, Alexandra decided to **terminate** her work for his campaign.

Even though some people thought it was a laughing matter, James talked about it with extreme **sobriety**.

exploit	to take advantage of; to use selfishly for one's own ends
integrity	honesty; moral uprightness
novice	a person who is new at something
revere	to regard with awe
satiate	satisfy fully

slander untruthful spoken attack on someone's reputation
sobriety being quiet or serious
succumb to give way to superior force
terminate bring to an end
truncate shorten by cutting off
yearning deep longing

On Trial For Your Life

Your honor, the **defendant** is obviously lying; his nose is getting longer.

I ask that this man's **testimony** about the accident be stricken from the record because it disagrees with mine.

In **rebuttal** of the prosecution's case against me, I would like to call my mother to the stand.

I would like to **debunk** this young woman's claim that I am her mother; I have never seen her before in my life.

He is a known **truant**; last week, he showed up at school only twice.

The governor is going to **repeal** the death penalty, but he wants to wait until after your execution.

If I have steak for my last meal, would that **preclude** my having lobster as well?

The man **swindled** innocent people by persuading them to buy **tracts** of land that were underwater at high tide.

It is **patently** obvious that I won't get a fair trial in this state.

The **tacit** opinion of this court is that you are a crybaby, but of course we wouldn't say that to your face.

It is my **unbiased** and **objective** opinion that you are not good at anything.

The judge has decided to **void** the lower court's decision to set you free, and instead send you to jail for 144 years.

My client is basically **innocuous**. He wouldn't harm a fly—unless the fly really provoked him.

We are asking that she be held without bail because she has been **elusive** in the past.

I don't know why you waste your time arguing with me. My reasoning is always **infallible**.

I find your arguments to be **trite**—almost clichés.

I **infer** from your gagging noises that you don't think much of my conclusion.

May I raise one small **quibble**? Your mother wears army boots.

debunk	to expose the falseness of something or someone
defendant	someone who has been accused of committing a crime
elusive	cleverly avoiding or escaping
infallible	unable to be proven wrong
infer	conclude by reasoning
innocuous	causing or intending little or no harm
objective	not affected by personal feelings
quibble	*v*: to make a minor objection *n*: a small objection
patent	obvious, readily visible
preclude	to make impossible
rebuttal	reply to a criticism or challenge
repeal	to take back a law or other decision
swindle	to cheat out of money or property
tacit	implied, not stated outright
testimony	statement in support of something, often under oath
tract	a piece of land
trite	overused, lacking freshness
truant	someone who cuts school or neglects his or her duties
unbiased	without prejudice
void	to invalidate

The "Artsy" Book Report

The **aesthetic** sensibility demonstrated by the writing took my breath away.

I found the book to be so **stylized** that I couldn't empathize with the characters. The central **paradox** of this book is that any publisher would be foolish enough to print it in the first place.

The author offers a rich **mosaic** of different immigrants' lives all seamlessly bound together.

The meaning of the passage is almost totally **opaque**— we don't understand the character's motivation, or even what happened to her.

Before I comment on the book's themes, I will begin with a long **synopsis** of the plot.

Each **stanza** of the poem contains three lines, none of which rhyme.

My **thesis** is that the author is in search of his inner child; to prove my point I have written this 900 page manuscript.

At the end of the book, the author returns to the scene that began the book, thus giving a pleasing **symmetry** to the work.

The **phenomena** described in the book are less interesting than the unseen forces that produced them.

While it could be said that *Topics in Linguistic Phonetics* is an **esoteric** book, I for one found it to be a good read.

His art was a **synthesis** of ancient Greek and modern styles.

aesthetic	pertaining to beauty
esoteric	known only by a select few
mosaic	a picture made of small pieces of stone or glass
opaque	not transparent, hard to understand
paradox	something that seems to contradict itself
phenomena	occurrences, facts, or observable circumstances
phonetics	the study of sounds in a language
stanza	section of a poem
stylized	in a particular style, often an unrealistic one
symmetry	balanced proportions
synopsis	plot summary
synthesis	the combining of separate parts to form a whole
thesis	unproven theory; long research paper

At the Game

The spirit of the match was **marred** when the home team refused to shake hands with the visitors.

If we are going to win, we have to **obliterate** their defense.

We must **vanquish** the opposing team in the final quarter.

We're behind by 22 points in the fourth quarter; it's looking **ominous**.

The offsetting penalties **nullified** each other.

The personal foul **negated** the touchdown, and the play had to be done over.

I had a **premonition** about this game so I bet my life-savings.

The offense is looking **sluggish**—someone had better wake them up.

You know, the cast on his leg has barely affected his **mobility**.

There is **speculation** that he might be traded to the Bulls.

The **supremacy** of our volleyball team was evident as they handily defeated their opponents.

The cheerleaders **synchronized** their movements so that they finished at precisely the same instant.

Lisa was an **unheralded** volleyball player until she won the big game for us; now, of course, we treat her like a star.

The coach was suspended from the NCAA for **unethical** practices.

Their victory over State University was **unprecedented**; in 30 years of competition, State University has always won.

marred	impaired the perfection of
mobility	ability to move or be moved
negate	to destroy the validity of something
nullify	to make invalid or worthless
obliterate	to wipe out, remove all traces
ominous	signaling something evil is about to happen
premonition	a feeling that something is about to happen
sluggish	lacking energy
speculation	the act of thinking about or pondering something
supremacy	the state of being supreme, or having the most power
synchronize	to cause to occur at the same time
unethical	having bad moral principles
unheralded	unnoticed or unappreciated
unprecedented	without parallel
vanquish	overpower an enemy completely

Homework Excuses (My Canine Devoured It)

Do not **condemn** me for not doing my homework, Ms. Cornwell! There are **mitigating** circumstances: I felt it would be **detrimental** to my development if I were to be tied down to the mindless **conformity** of such **conventional** homework.

I also thought that so much typing might **exacerbate** the injury to my wrist.

The book was so **opaque** that I didn't understand a word. Moreover, it was so **soporific** that I couldn't stay awake while reading it.

I know this may sound **implausible**, but as an alternative form of homework I wrote a 50-page paper. I know that it contains a few errors—after all, no one is **infallible**.

Not a single bit of it was **plagiarized**, I wrote it all myself. Although it does contain one paragraph which could be considered a **pastiche**.

condemn	to express strong disapproval of
conformity	the act of becoming similar or identical to
conventional	traditional, mundane
detrimental	causing damage or harm
exacerbate	to make worse
implausible	not possible, not imaginable
infallible	unable to be proven wrong
mitigate	to make less severe
opaque	not transparent, hard to understand

pastiche piece of music, writing, or art combining several different sources or styles
plagiarist A person who presents someone else's work as his or her own
soporific causing sleep

Responses to Parents

But Mom, the music is practically **inaudible** right now.

An 11 o'clock curfew is so **provincial**.

(or if you really want to impress them...)

This punishment is **tantamount** to **persecution**.

Okay, so I didn't take out the garbage, but don't worry; I'll **rectify** the situation tomorrow.

My room is my **sanctuary**. Please leave.

I'm not active; I'm **slothful**.

Please don't **provoke** me now; I'm feeling very **vulnerable**.

I hereby **renounce** all blood-ties to you.

inaudible too quiet to be heard
persecution tormenting a person because of his or her beliefs
provincial having a narrow scope
provoke anger, arouse, bring to action
rectify fix, correct
renounce to give up or put aside
sanctuary a safe place or a room for worship
slothful lazy
tantamount equivalent in effect or meaning
vulnerable capable of being hurt

Writing the College Essay

There are many examples that testify to my **indomitable** spirit; for example, when I stubbed my toe before a big test, I went right ahead and took that test, even though I was in tremendous pain. I could have gone to the nurse to get an excuse, but my **innate integrity** would not allow me to take the easy way out.

Although I am only 17 years old, I am considered a **pioneer** in microbiology, having made many important discoveries in the field. Indeed, some colleagues have been tempted to call me **omniscient** since I seem to have an almost encyclopedic grasp of the subject matter. However, my modesty always makes me tell them that they must **temper** their hero-worship. After all, even if my genius makes any modesty **superfluous**, I still **strive** to be a regular guy, who just happens to have the **vitality** of a superhero and the **virtue** of Mother Teresa.

indomitable unable to be subdued or overcome
innate existing in a person since birth; part of the character of something
integrity honesty; moral uprightness
omniscient having complete knowledge
pioneer *n.* a leader in a field *v.* to lead the way in a field
strive try hard, make a major effort
superfluous unnecessary
temper to moderate, to make less extreme
virtue moral excellence
vitality energy, liveliness

The Job Interview

My worst attribute? I'm too **meticulous**; no detail is too small for me to keep track of.

My work methods are very **methodical** and **systematic**; I always start with task A and then move to task B.

No task is too **mundane** or **monotonous** for me, and I'll always perform it with a smile.

May I ask how much you paid my **predecessor**?

Give me your biggest problems and I'll solve them. I'm very **resourceful**.

I actually like **subordinate** roles; I don't like responsibility.

I see myself as a **utility** player. I can fit into lots of situations. I'm very **versatile**.

Energy? Are you kidding? I have lots of **vigor**. I'm just full of **zeal**.

So, what's the **prevailing** wage at this Gap outlet?

methodical orderly; having a set system
meticulous very careful; attentive to details
mundane ordinary or commonplace
monotonous boring; unvarying in tone or content
predecessor a person who precedes another in an office or a position
prevailing generally accepted; having superior power
resourceful able to find solutions
subordinate placed in a lower order or rank

systematic regular
utility usefulness
versatile capable of doing many things well
vigor energy, vitality
zeal enthusiasm and intensity

Alternate Words for "Cool"

"So what do you think of Lisa?"

"She's totally cool."

"Could you be more specific?"

If you think she's clever: "She's **witty**."

If she's clever in a sophisticated sort of way: "She's really **urbane**."

If she's clever in a dry sort of way: "She's **wry**."

If she's really lively: She's really **vivid**."

If she's really important: "She's **vital**."

If she's new and different: "She's really **novel**."

If her comments are short and to the point: "She's **succinct**."

If she's never ruffled: "She's really **serene**."

If she never gives up: "She's very **resolute**."

If she can always get out of gym class: "She's **ingenious**."

If she goes beyond all known limits: "She's really **transcendent**."

ingenuity cleverness; originality
novel original, new and different
resolute strongly determined
serene calm, peaceful
succinct brief, concise
transcendent going beyond known limits
urbane highly sophisticated
vital full of energy; necessary for life
vivid sharp, intense; making an impression on the senses
witty clever or amusing
wry dryly humorous

You're in Love with Him/Her, So You Have to Try to Explain Him/Her to Your Friends

It's not that he can't talk, he's just **taciturn**.

It's not that he doesn't have an opinion, he's just **reticent**.

She didn't insult you on purpose, it was **unwitting**.

He's not **arrogant**, he's just very confident.

It's not that she hates the entire human race, she's just a little **cynical**.

I'm sure it wasn't **deliberate**. It must have been unintentional.

He's not a **dupe**. He's just very naive.

She's not **gullible**. She's just very innocent.

She's not a **miser**, she's just extremely careful with her money.

She's not **obsessive**. She just happens to like arranging her dolls in exact size order.

He's not a **recluse**. He just enjoys his solitude.

It's not that he isn't passionate. He's **stoic**.

He isn't exactly **strident**, he's just a little grating.

It's not that she's **vengeful**, she just never forgets a slight.

I admit he's a little **vociferous**, but to my knowledge, his **tirades** have never broken anyone's eardrum.

She isn't **verbose**, she just uses a lot of words.

She isn't **sullen**, she's mysterious.

He isn't **torpid** or **slothful**, he's just kind of tranquil.

She isn't a **traitor**, she's just not very loyal.

It's not that he's unfaithful. He just likes a lot of **diversity**.

It's not that he's **indecisive**, he just has trouble making up his mind.

She isn't **erratic**, she simply has her own way of doing things.

It's not that she has no personality, she is just **tactful**.

She isn't nosy, she's just very **inquisitive**.

We're a great match; her **tranquility** offsets my nervous personality.

She's not unfocused, she just has **vague** career plans.

arrogance	overconfidence
cynicism	the belief that all human action is motivated by selfishness
deliberate	*adj.* intentional, well thought out *v.* to consider carefully
diversity	the state of having different elements
dupe	a person easily deceived
erratic	unpredictably eccentric

gullible	easily deceived
indecision	inability to decide
inquisitive	curious
miser	one who saves greedily
obsessive	overly preoccupied
recluse	someone who lives in seclusion
reticent	untalkative, shy, reluctant to speak
slothful	lazy
strident	harsh, grating
stoic	not affected by passion or feeling
sullen	sad, sulky
tactful	saying or doing the proper thing
taciturn	being of few words
tirade	a long, harsh, often abusive speech
torpid	without energy, sluggish
traitor	one who betrays a person, cause, or country
tranquillity	calmness, peacefulness
unwitting	unaware
vague	not precise, unclear
vengeful	wanting or seeking revenge
verbosity	the use of too many words
vociferous	loud

Baby-sitting

Hello, 911? Is there an **antidote** if someone just drank a whole bottle of Maalox?

Young man, your **impudence** is not respectful to someone who is as old as I am.

Young lady, you are **incorrigible**; they are going to lock you up and throw away the key.

Don't write on the wall, Timmy! That magic marker is **indelible**.

You may be your parents' sole **heir**, but if you don't get down from that refrigerator, you won't live to inherit.

Don't **provoke** me, young man.

If you and your sister want to engage in sibling **rivalry**, it's okay with me so long as there are no scars on your bodies.

Jessica screams all night, so I may need something **soporific** to **subdue** my anxiety and get some sleep. . . something strong enough to **stupefy** me.

Don't try to **undermine** my authority!

You **wily** little brat. I can tell you're still awake.

antidote remedy for a poison
heir a person who inherits another's belongings
impudence bold disrespect or rudeness
incorrigible not capable of being reformed
indelible incapable of being erased
provoke anger, arouse, bring to action
rivalry an ongoing competition
soporific causing sleep
stupefy to make less alert
subdued quiet, controlled, lacking in intensity
undermine to injure or destroy underhandedly
wily artful, cunning, deceitful, sly

Alternate Words for "Bogus"

"So what do you think of Dave?"

"He's totally bogus."

"Could you be more specific?"

If he's narrow-minded, he's just very **parochial**.

If he just doesn't matter, he's **irrelevant**.

If he's really ordinary, he's **mediocre** or **mundane**.

If he's got nothing to offer, he's **meager**.

If he's really boring, he's **monotonous**.

If he's gloomy, he's **morose**.

If he's been superseded by someone else, he's **obsolete**.

If he's no longer relevant, he's **extraneous**.

If he has no moral principles, he's **unethical**.

If he makes you nervous, he's **unnerving**.

If he's lacking freshness, he's **trite**.

If he's not in good taste, he's **unseemly**.

If he's not a solid character, he's **unsound**.

If he isn't a serious person, he's **superficial**.

If no one knows who he is, he's **obscure**.

extraneous not pertinent or relevant
irrelevant not necessary or important to the matter at hand
meager lacking in amount or quality; poor
mediocrity ordinariness; lack of distinction
monotonous boring; unvarying in tone or content

morose gloomy; ill-tempered
mundane ordinary or commonplace
obscure not known; difficult to understand
obsolete outdated
parochial having a narrow scope
superficial near the surface; slight
trite overused, lacking freshness
unseemly unbecoming
unsound not solid; not well founded; not healthy
unethical having bad moral principles
unnerving upsetting; causing nervousness

Meeting Royalty

Well, your highness, it's been a **tumultuous** year what with all the scandals.

Are you planning to disinherit any of your **heirs**?

Do you **sanction** your son's behavior?

Have you considered imposing **sanctions** on your son's behavior?

I hear that to be queen of England you have to be willing to wear **ghastly** clothes.

When a **monarch** has relatives like yours, it must be tough to keep your sense of humor.

The constant **lampoons** in the newspapers must be very hard to laugh at when you are their subject.

With the King's death, I imagine there is very little **levity** in the palace right now.

Tell me, your highness, has anyone tried to **usurp** the throne lately?

I've never met such a **lofty magnate** as yourself. Could I have your autograph?

Actually, I'm very **prominent** in Omaha, Nebraska; everybody knows me there.

Long may you **reign**, but could I have that scepter when you kick the bucket?

Are you thinking of **repudiating** your claim to rule America?

Would you take a picture of me posing with this **sentinel**?

These journalists seem to be **ubiquitous**; can't you get rid of them?

ghastly shockingly frightful
heir a person who inherits another's belongings
lampoon sharp satire
levity lightness; lacking seriousness
lofty having great height or a stately manner
magnate a person of great influence in a particular field

monarch	a ruler; a king, queen, or emperor
prominent	standing out, important
reign	*n.* having supreme power *v.* to rule
repudiate	to cast off or disown; to refuse to acknowledge
sanction	*v.* to give permission *n.* a coercive measure designed to make a person or persons comply
sentinel	a guard, a watchman
tumultuous	characterized by a noisy uproar
ubiquitous	being everywhere at the same time
usurp	to seize power by force

Getting Religion

The two religious sects have gone in **divergent** directions, but they still meet twice a year in Rome to try to **reconcile** their differences.

The **tenets** of his faith included turning the other cheek.

The **theologian** had been studying religion for more than 20 years.

She was a **pious** person who spent much time in prayer.

The **fundamental** beliefs of the church have not changed in 500 years.

Having been raised in an agnostic household, he was unfamiliar with religious **jargon**.

There was great **lamentation** when the Buddhist priest died.

In a recent **purgation**, one religious **sect** was invited to leave the main body because of doctrinal differences.

Many religions portray hell as a huge **conflagration** that will burn for all eternity.

conflagration	a widespread fire
divergent	moving in different directions from a common point
fundamental	basic, essential
jargon	words used by people in a particular field of work
lamentation	an expression of sorrow or deep regret
pious	having reverence for a god
purgation	the process of getting rid of impurities
reconcile	to settle a problem
sect	a subgroup of a religion; faction
tenet	idea or belief
theologian	one who studies religion

How to Succeed in Business

Your **proposal** for a new headquarters is too expensive.

Our board of directors voted **unanimously** against the proposal.

We were **uniform** in our hatred of your plan.

Our **agenda** now is to find an alternate proposal.

Using both proposals would be **redundant**.

The **blueprint** for our new building calls for 40 stories.

This is a **comprehensive** plan that covers every eventuality.

We do not want the government to **regulate** our industry. We prefer to police ourselves.

We are hoping that the **stimulus** of a cash infusion will turn our company profitable.

Our results are **verifiable**; an accounting firm has gone over our books and pronounced them accurate.

Our results are not **theoretical**; they are based on hard evidence.

There may be some **residual** ill-feeling from our workers after we cut their salaries by 40 percent.

agenda a schedule of a meeting
blueprint a detailed outline or plan for a building
comprehensive including everything; complete
proposal an offer or consideration for acceptance
redundant characterized by unnecessary repetition of words or ideas
regulate to control or direct by some particular method
residual describing the part left over
stimulus something that causes a reaction
theoretical not proven true, existing only as an idea
unanimity complete agreement
uniform alike, identical
verifiable able to be proven true

The Hit Parade (in alphabetical order)

abridge to shorten
abstemious sparing in the use of food or drink
abhor to loathe or detest
aesthetic pertaining to beauty
agenda a schedule of a meeting
ambiguous unclear; having more than one meaning
amorphous having no shape
antidote remedy for a poison
apathy lack of interest or caring
arrogance overconfidence
blueprint a detailed outline or plan for a building
comprehensive including everything, complete
condemn to express strong disapproval of
conflagration a widespread fire
conformity the act of becoming similar or identical to

conventional	traditional, mundane
cynicism	the belief that all human action is motivated by selfishness
debunk	to expose the falseness
defendant	someone who has been accused of committing a crime
detrimental	causing damage or harm
deliberate	*adj.* intentional, well thought out *v.* to consider carefully
divergent	moving in different directions from a common point
diversity	the state of being different or having different elements
dupe	a person easily deceived
elusive	cleverly avoiding or escaping
erratic	unpredictably eccentric
esoteric	known only by a select few
exacerbate	to make worse
exemplary	serving as an example; commendable
exploit	to take advantage of, to use selfishly for one's own ends
extraneous	not pertinent or relevant
fluid	capable of flowing; changing readily, as a plan
fundamental	basic, essential
ghastly	shockingly frightful
gullible	easily deceived
hiatus	a break or lapse in continuity
heir	a person who inherits another's belongings
hoard	to accumulate or stash away
implausible	not possible, not imaginable
impudence	bold disrespect or rudeness
inaudible	too quiet to be heard
incorrigible	not capable of being reformed
indecision	inability to decide
indelible	incapable of being erased
indifference	lack of interest, feeling, or opinion
indomitable	unable to be subdued or overcome
infallible	unable to be proven wrong
inferred	concluded by reasoning
ingenuity	cleverness; originality
injurious	causing damage or loss
innate	existing in a person since birth; part of the character of something
innocuous	causing or intending little or no harm
inquisitive	curious
integrity	honesty; moral uprightness
irrelevant	not necessary or important to the matter at hand
jargon	words used by people in a particular field of work
lamentation	an expression of sorrow or deep regret
lampoon	sharp satire

levity	lightness; lacking seriousness
lofty	having great height or a stately manner
lurid	gruesome, melodramatic, shocking
magnate	a person of great influence in a particular field
marred	impaired the perfection of
meager	lacking in amount or quality; poor
mediocrity	ordinariness, lack of distinction
methodical	orderly, having a set system
meticulous	very careful, attentive to details
migrate	to move from one place to another
miser	one who saves greedily
mitigate	to make less severe
mobility	ability to move or be moved
monarch	a ruler; a king, queen or emperor
monotonous	boring; unvarying in tone or content
morose	gloomy; ill-tempered
mosaic	a picture made of small pieces of stone or glass
mundane	ordinary or commonplace
negate	to destroy the validity of something
novel	original, new and different
novice	a person who is new at something
nullify	to make invalid or worthless
obliterate	to wipe out, remove all traces
obscure	not known; difficult to understand
obsessive	overly preoccupied
objective	not affected by personal feelings
obsolete	outdated
ominous	signaling something evil is about to happen
omniscient	having complete knowledge
opaque	not transparent; hard to understand
paradox	something that seems to contradict itself
parochial	having a narrow scope
pastiche	piece of music, writing, or art combining several different sources or styles
patent	obvious, readily visible
paucity	small amount or number
penchant	a strong taste or liking
persecution	tormenting a person because of his or her beliefs
phenomena	occurrences, facts, or observable circumstances
philanthropist	someone who gives to worthy causes
phonetics	the study of sounds in a language
pioneer	*n.* a leader in a field *v.* to lead the way in a field
pious	having reverence for a god
plagiarist	A person who presents someone else's work as his or her own
plateau	a condition of neither growth nor decline

precarious	unstable, insecure
preclude	to make impossible
predecessor	a person who precedes another in an office or a position
premonition	a feeling that something is about to happen
presumptuous	bold to the point of rudeness
prevailing	generally accepted; having superior power
prevalent	in general use or acceptance
prodigal	wasteful
prominent	standing out, important
promontory	a high point of land projecting into the sea
proposal	an offer or consideration or acceptance
provincial	having a narrow scope
provoke	anger, arouse, bring to action
purgation	the process of getting rid of impurities
quarry	a large open pit from which stone is cut
quibble	*v.* to make a minor objection *n.* a small objection
raconteur	skilled storyteller
rebuttal	reply to a criticism or challenge
recant	to take back
recluse	someone who lives in seclusion
reconcile	to settle a problem
rectify	fix, correct
redundant	characterized by unnecessary repetition of words or ideas
reminiscence	a story of past experiences
regulate	to control or direct by some particular method
reign	having supreme power *v.* to rule
reiteration	saying or doing something repeatedly
renounce	to give up or put aside
repeal	to take back a law or other decision
repertoire	supply of songs, stories, skills or devices
replete	gorged with food, sated
repudiate	to cast off or disown; to refuse to acknowledge
residual	describing the part that is left over
resourceful	able to find solutions
resolute	strongly determined
reticent	untalkative, shy, reluctant to speak
retort	*v.* to reply sharply *n.* a sharp reply
revere	to regard with awe
revelation	striking realization
rivalry	an ongoing competition
sanctuary	a safe place or a room for worship
sanction	*v.* to give permission *n.* a coercive measure designed to make a person or persons comply
satiate	satisfy fully
sect	a subgroup of a religion; faction

sentinel a guard, a watchman
serene calm, peaceful
skeptical showing doubt and disbelief
slander untruthful spoken attack on someone's reputation
slothful lazy
sluggish lacking energy
sobriety being quiet or serious
solidarity fellowship between members of a group
solitude the state of living or being alone
soporific causing sleep
speculation the act of thinking about or pondering something
spendthrift a person who spends money wastefully
stanza section of a poem
stimulus something that causes a reaction
strident harsh, grating
strive try hard; make a major effort
stylized in a particular style, often an unrealistic one
stoic not affected by passion or feeling
stupefy to make less alert
subdued quiet, controlled, lacking in intensity
subordinate placed in a lower order or rank
subtle hardly noticeable
sullen sad, sulky
succinct brief, concise
succumb to give way to superior force
superficial near the surface; slight
superfluous unnecessary
supremacy the state of being supreme, or having the most power
surfeit excess, overindulgence
suppleness ability to bend easily; limberness
swindle to cheat out of money or property
synopsis plot summary
synthesis the combining of separate parts to form a whole
symmetry balanced proportions
synchronize to cause to occur at the same time
synthesis the combining of separate parts to form a whole
systematic regular
tacit implied, not stated outright
taciturn being of few words
tactful saying or doing the proper thing
taint to affect with something harmful; contaminate
tantamount equivalent in effect or meaning
taper gradually decrease, grow smaller at one end; dwindle
temper to moderate, to make less extreme
temperament one's emotional nature

tenet	idea or belief
terminate	bring to an end
terrestrial	having to do with the earth
testimony	statement in support of something, often under oath
theologian	one who studies religion
theoretical	not proven true, existing only as an idea
thesis	unproven theory; long research paper
tirade	a long, harsh, often abusive speech
torpid	without energy, sluggish
tract	a piece of land
traitor	one who betrays a person, cause, or country
tranquillity	calmness, peacefulness
transcendent	going beyond known limits
trite	overused, lacking freshness
truant	someone who cuts school or neglects his or her duties
truncate	shorten by cutting off
tumultuous	characterized by a noisy uproar
unbiased	without prejudice
ubiquitous	being everywhere at the same time
unanimity	complete agreement
undermine	to injure or destroy underhandedly
unethical	having bad moral principles
unheralded	unnoticed or unappreciated
uniform	alike, identical
unnerving	upsetting; causing nervousness
unprecedented	without parallel
unseemly	unbecoming
unsound	not solid; not well founded; not healthy
unwitting	unaware
urbane	highly sophisticated
usurp	to seize power by force
utility	usefulness
vacillation	wavering; going back and forth
vagary	inconsistent or unpredictable action
vague	not precise; unclear
vane	a device that measures wind direction
vanquish	overpower an enemy completely
vegetation	plant life
veiled	covered or concealed
vengeful	wanting or seeking revenge
vent	express with emotion
verbosity	the use of too many words
uniform	alike, identical
verifiable	able to be proven true
versatile	capable of doing many things well

virtue	moral excellence
vigor	energy, vitality
vital	full of energy, necessary for life
vitality	energy, liveliness
vivid	sharp, intense, making an impression on the senses
vociferous	loud
void	to invalidate
vulnerable	capable of being hurt
wallow	to indulge in a particular state of mind
wariness	cautiousness
wharf	a structure built to extend from the land out over the water
whimsical	eccentric; unpredictable
wily	artful, cunning, deceitful, sly
witty	clever or amusing
wry	dryly humorous
yearning	a deep longing
zealous	very enthusiastic and intense

Great! You're almost done with vocabulary. Just one more thing—turn to the Appendix at the back of the book. There you will find a set of flashcards to practice with whenever you have an extra minute or two. We left a few blank so you can write down words and definitions that you have the most trouble with. (Don't mention it.)

ABOUT THE AUTHOR

After attending Dartmouth and Columbia, Geoff Martz joined The Princeton Review as a teacher and writer. He is the author or co-author of *Cracking the GMAT, Cracking the ACT, Cracking the GED, Paying for College, How To Survive Without Your Parents' Money*, and the CD-ROM software program, *Inside the SAT*.

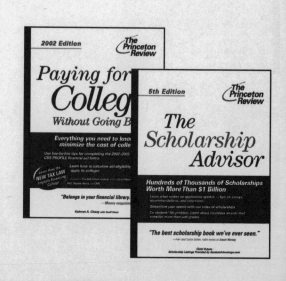

THE PRINCETON REVIEW NETWORK

The Princeton Review wants to provide you with the most up-to-date information you need whether you are preparing to take a test or apply to school. If you are usuing our books outside of the United States and have questions or comments, or simply want more information on our courses and the services The Princeton Review offers, please contact one of the following offices nearest to you.

- HONG KONG 852-517-3016
- JAPAN (Tokyo) 8133-463-1343
- KOREA (Seoul) 822-795-3028
- MEXICO CITY 011-525-358-0855
- PAKISTAN (Lahore) 92-42-872-315
- SAUDI ARABIA 413-548-6849 (a U.S. based number)
- SPAIN (Madrid) 341-446-5541
- TAIWAN (Taipei) 886-27511293